Pine Creek Church Library

How to Use
the Power of
Your Word

STELLA TERRILL MANN

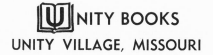
UNITY BOOKS
UNITY VILLAGE, MISSOURI

CONTENTS

Message to the Reader

The general purpose of this book:

The general purpose of this book is the same as that of my three books (Dodd, Mead) which preceded it—to help the individual to help himself in working with his everyday problems, to obtain his highest heart's desire, and to promote his soul growth through a knowledge and use of spiritual laws. My own life having been saved through prayer some years ago, I feel that the least I can do in gratitude is to continue to share even the little that I have learned.

The specific purpose of this volume is to continue where the last book left off. Here we take up the spiritual power of the *human spoken word*, which includes the *power of thought* and the laws that govern the Power of decree.

In the three previous books we studied first the laws of desire, or reaching out and asking, in "Change Your Life through Prayer." The law of love and the power of attraction were covered in "Change Your Life through Love." The law of faith believe-receive, and the power of action were studied in "Change Your Life through Faith and Work."

The casual reader need not go into the three previous books in order to understand and use the laws and the power discussed in this book. But the serious student who is earnestly seeking to understand today's modern world and to live a life of peace, confidence, health, success, and soul growth will want to read the others in order to get the most out of this present volume. There is no way to separate the laws in life and living. The total of the spiritual laws add up to what Jesus termed truth, or God's will. Truth means things as they are, fact found out. And just as Jesus explained, truth when known and followed results in freedom for the individual, freedom from fear, sin, sickness, poverty, unhappiness, and death. If the laws Jesus taught will work for the individual, then they will work for the world of men.

The hope of this book:

The hope of this book is that readers everywhere will take to heart the truth I have tried to put into it and make use of it in their daily living. It comes from the Bible, modern science, years of experience, and answer to prayer. If only one person is helped, uplifted, to *the point of action*, then this book will not have been written in vain. But, oh, if one should be so inspired as to set forth on such a work for humanity that ages after people would rise up and call him blessed, then my own life will not have been in vain. For that is my greatest heart's desire—to help others lift the consciousness level of all men.

My thanks are due:

In the highest sense, I did not write this book. I am but a channel through which the great creative Spirit of the universe works. The people whose case histories appear here, the writers of the books of the Bible, and many writers of books of modern science and religion are the real authors. I am a teacher, and so important is the subject I try to teach that I feel justified, duty bound, to drink freely from the fountains of wisdom of the truly great ones.

To all of you who have written me, presenting your problems, asking questions, giving me encouragement and your prayers, to you who filled the halls where I have lectured and to you readers who never have contacted me, but nevertheless have given me your support in thought and prayer, I say thank you from my heart.

You have helped me more than you can ever know.

The greatest religious movement that the world has ever seen has begun. Will it go on until man reaches the complete freedom which the Christian religion predicts, or will it be cut short by the machines of science?

That depends upon you and me—individuals—and how we will use the power God has given us. The fact that you have this book in your hand is proof that you are on the creative Christian side. As you read, listen to the prayers between the lines. Listen to the voice of the Spirit, the Comforter that hovers over the earth, and you will not only understand what I tried to say (but can never fully say), but you will put aside all your fears and take up a line of action.

God bless you!

STELLA TERRILL MANN

Pasadena, Calif.

CIRCLE OF PRAYER

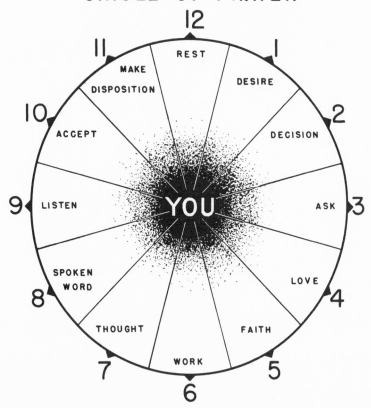

The Power of Your Tongue

By your words you will be justified, and by your words you will be condemned (Matthew 12:37).

I will condemn you out of your own mouth (Luke 19:22).

The Bible is a textbook on the powers of man and the spiritual laws under which they operate. It tells us that we come to earth filled with a power we can't turn off. It is the power which resides in us as a Self, or a Word of God. It is called the Power of decree. We use it every time we think or speak.

Fear, sin, sickness, suffering, and poverty are results of a guilty or an innocent wrong use of the Power of decree.

Happiness, success, good health, joy, peace, prosperity, abundance, and all other obtained good desires are the result of an unconscious or a deliberate, well-planned, and carried-out right use of the Power of decree.

We are using this Power constantly all day long, all our life long, with results that turn out to be constructive or destructive, bringing us the good we desire or the evil we do not want. We must, therefore, *learn how consciously to use* our everyday desires, thoughts, words, and belief for good, or be destroyed by the mistakes we make and the evil we consciously or unconsciously form. This is because the Power works according to spiritual laws that are unfailing.

The Bible is filled with references to the power that

resides in our everyday spoken words and thoughts. It teaches us how to use this power correctly and warns us that death itself is the extreme result of its wrong use. But it takes study, downright digging, to find and assemble the Bible truths. Few people in this workaday world have the time to read even that which the scholars have learned and put together for us. It takes time and thought to separate and prove one point of Truth by testing it again and again and throughout the Bible comparing it with other references and examples of the same Truth until the real meaning has been established. This book will not replace such careful study, which the serious student will want to do for himself, but with a few terms now we can see how these truths work out in life.

To avoid confusion of terms, used in the examples following and throughout this book:

Power, capitalized, denotes God at work. But *power*, lower case, denotes man's ability to turn on and use God's Power.

Word, capitalized, means the divine individual in each of us, that Self which God created, which Jesus called "the Father within," and which the Bible often refers to as the Son of God or the "only begotten" of God.

Key means the keynote of using the Power on higher levels, which is faith. "According to your faith be it done to you" is the key to the use of all spiritual laws.

We will pick up our facts, define our further terms as we go along. But right now, we will learn most by seeing the Power of the Word in action. Here are examples from my files:

An ambitious and somewhat callous businessman who had taken some courses in sales psychology had learned a low level of the use of the power of his word and had used it wrongly. He employed it with a set purpose to overcome the "sales resistance" of his fellow men. He worked up tremendous self-confidence in his ability, which carried him to a high financial success. He began to think of himself as invincible.

"Whatever I make up my mind to do, I *can* do," he told his wife arrogantly, very proud of his cunning. "I can get anything I want in life."

The wife was unhappy about some of his success and often pleaded with him to change his ways. "You are causing others to suffer," she would object. "That is wrong."

But the man excused his acts by saying, "It is a law of nature." They lived near the ocean. He used to tell his wife: "Out there it is eat or be eaten. The smartest fish survives. The poor sucker gets taken in. It is a law of life, the way we learn. Those fellows [his business associates, the gullible public, his prospective victims] are my natural prey. Look, honey," he would say, when his wife argued with him, "we have everything we want; we live high because I have learned how to use my mind power. I have a master mind. I can do anything I say I can do! I just decide what I want and then I go after it, hammer and tongs. I have a right to take others in. You ought to be proud of me, honey. Don't you know that any fellow bigger than I am will take me in if I am fool enough to let him?"

Then one day a man he thought of as just "another poor fish, another sucker," turned out to be a man-eating shark, who beached him, to use his phraseology. The aggressor became a victim. He lost all he had accumulated in wealth, prestige, self-confidence, and the love of his wife. He also lost his freedom. He was sent to prison.

Now, let's take it apart and see how the law works:

The man was not interested in learning the spiritual laws of the universe. He did not know or did not care about the highest of them, the law of love. But since all the laws are unfailing, the man's end was in sight from

11

the beginning because his purpose was wrong. We are born with a conscience and, no matter how often we violate it, we cannot kill it. The man's inner voice, the "judge" that is always on the bench, added to his wife's words, *led him into the situation* that proved so disastrous for him. Seen from the highest point of view, he had talked himself into prison.

The next point to consider:

This is a moral universe. It is run by law and order. None of us can harm the universe. We can harm others who are in tune with us, on our level, and do not know how to protect themselves. We can and do harm ourselves even unto death. We are always setting such traps for ourselves as that man did, when our purpose is wrong. The very same Power alive within our human word which we use against others will be used against us. Not because the Power itself turns against us. It cannot. The Power is a power, an intelligent force, not a person. But we ourselves set it into motion to hurt us by our very own word. What we thought was a pruning hook for us to use to "trim" someone else, becomes a sword that runs us through. The hidden sense of guilt produces fear. We may hide the fear from others, and bluster it out for ourselves, but the law works and what we fear comes upon us. Fear is a *form of decree.* It is a forceful way of saying "Let there be!"

The final point to consider is this: The spiritual law says that "As he [man] thinketh in his heart so *is* he." We always decree from our heart. Our heart means the total belief, the thought-collective which we are as an individual. That man decreed from his heart—from what he believed about life, man, God, and their relationship.

We worry and fret our lives away not realizing that two-thirds of all our earth problems already have been solved for us. The Power, or ability, is already there, awaiting our human spoken word of decree—our throwing of the switch. We cannot be reminded of this simple fact too often; it is in our very own mouth. We do not have to create the power or beg for the privilege of using it. It is, and it is ours, right now. All the materials and principles that we shall ever need to make heaven on earth are here, waiting for us to wake up and learn how to use the one to put the other together. By this process man has put together radios, television, and atomic bombs of our day. Tomorrow, we shall go much further and use principles for direct action on material substances. Meantime, let us remember that two-thirds of our work has been done. Earth is a practice field for humanity. It is a school in which we are to learn the remaining one-third by our own efforts.

The failures in life do not know about the power of their decree; much less do they know how to use it correctly. They speak from a heart that seems to have no knowledge of love or of spiritual laws. But the law is no respecter of persons. It is always fulfilled to the last "jot and tittle."

Example:

Mrs. C—— was poor but she admired and longed for beautiful things for her home. One day her sister, very well-to-do, gave her a beautiful red glass vase.

"Oh, I just hate the thing," said Mrs. C——, when I admired the lovely vase. It was a most unusual one and quite expensive.

"Annie has such poor taste," said Mrs. C——, making a mouth of derision. It was a gesture of jealousy and hatred of her sister's more fortunate position in life.

Less than a week later Mrs. C—— accidentally dropped her lovely vase and it shattered into bits. When she told me about it, she showed genuine regret over the loss.

Let's see what we can learn from this:

Mrs. C—— did not really hate the vase. She hated what she felt was failure within herself. Her sister Annie was successful. She could buy presents. Mrs. C— was ungrateful and unloving. By her word (she was always wishing for beautiful things) she was justified—she received the gift. Ingratitude came from her heart into her thought and spoken words. So, by her word she had condemned her gift back to nothingness. Her actions automatically took charge of events. She stumbled (also a symbol) and bumped into a table so hard it upset her and she dropped the vase. She let it slip out of her hands into nothingness.

The words, acts, thoughts of the woman grew out of her heart. The heart, we must always remember, means the total attitudes, the thoughts and beliefs collective that we hold. Mrs. C—'s heart contained her hidden but very real attitude toward God, fellow man, and herself. Her heart contained jealousy, envy, ingratitude, lack of love of God, fellow man, and self. *Hate is a powerful way of saying* "Let there be!"

Let us then write the law and the warning into our working consciousness and remember it daily: "Keep your heart with all vigilance; from it flow the springs of life" (Proverbs 4:23).

Mrs. C— felt that God had discriminated against her. She called it bad luck. "I am always so unlucky," she often said. When she broke the vase, she complained to her husband that it was just her "usual bad luck. Wouldn't you know it would happen to me!"

But there is neither good nor bad luck in the universe. There is law and order.

"Annie gets all the breaks," Mrs. C— frequently declared. "Even before marriage, Annie was the lucky one. Then she married a man who makes a great deal of money, but look at my husband! We have a time getting by." All her life she had used her words to bring into her life that which she did not want. She used it to destroy the good she did desire. She complained so long and so bitterly about her husband that he left her. She did all this destruction from her heart out and never once realized the fact.

There are many people like Mrs. C——. Some of them destroy more than a red glass vase. They destroy the red corpuscles in their blood. They destroy their health, peace of mind, friendship, love, their very life on earth. Many wish to destroy other people because they wrongly think it is the only way in which they can get what they need and want. Yet all the while they could build a heaven on earth for themselves by using in the correct way the power God has given them.

Another example from my files shows yet another point of the truth we are now trying to learn:

A man who once had studied with me felt he knew his Bible and the truth pretty well, and left it after he started to earn a great deal of money. He became terribly worried about world affairs, problems of his business, unfair taxes, personalities in both high and low places and especially in his corner of the commercial world.

He lost sight of all the good, the true, the beautiful, and talked constantly of how "the world is going plumb to the dogs." He would say it with the full force of anger, frustration, and fear. He formerly had taken the long and right view of things. Now, having lost the right perspective (he had a change of heart, you see), he believed his fears would all come true. Through months his bitterness increased. "Everything is going plumb to the dogs" became a daily, almost an hourly, phrase.

One day, on a business trip, he took a wrong turn in a road and, before he noticed it, was on a narrow, rutty side road, little more than a lane, with no place to turn around.

The road became narrower and narrower, and he drove along feeling more and more concerned. Suddenly his car stalled. He got out to see what was wrong. He heard dogs barking. The sound frightened him so that he hurried back into his car. The dogs came on, a whole pack of them, barking, growling, behaving in a most savage and threatening manner. He closed the doors and windows of his car, growing more frightened by the instant. The dogs lunged at the doors, scratched the shiny finish on his fine new car, and "scared the living daylights out of me," the man reported.

Out of his subconscious (he said "the bottom of my heart where it had so long lain buried") came an old memory: "God is a very present help in time of trouble."

"O God, help me," the man called in desperation. "I ask it in the name and through the power of the Lord Jesus Christ," he added, remembering former instructions.

The dogs still raged and lunged. "I was so frightened," the man told me, "that a phrase you once gave me came back so clearly that I seemed to hear your actual, physical voice calmly saying to me, '*God is in this place.*'

"God *is* in this place!" the man declared aloud and with great feeling. Instantly his mind began to grow calmer. He started to recite Bible verses and affirmations he once had used. More dogs came to join the ugly, barking ones all around him. He closed his eyes and started to sing a hymn in order to blot out the sight and sound of the dogs.

Presently, the barking ceased. He continued to sing. A little later the dogs went away. The man got out of his car and onto his knees to thank God for comfort and deliverance. And before he got up off his knees "the thought came to me what to do about the car," he said.

After adjusting the car, the man drove ahead, found a clearing, turned the car around, and was soon back on the main highway. Once safe, he began to wonder about his frightening experience and to ask himself,

"How did I let myself in for that?"

The man had been an excellent student and knew his principles well. He formerly had made many demonstrations by intelligent use of spiritual laws. He drove along, asking himself the question over and over. Then he heard himself saying aloud, "Well, I said everything was going to the dogs, and that included my new car and myself. I simply had to go to the dogs, even though I had to lose myself off the main highway to find them. They did not leave their place and come to me on the highway. I detoured and went to them."

Wisely, the man took the lesson to be learned from his short journey into fear and began to get back onto the main highway of thinking and the right use of words. Today he says he knows perfectly well that the world is not going to the dogs, but that any individual may do so and some will, by speaking the word for it. As for himself, he knows that "the earth is the Lord's and the fulness thereof," and that the Lord of Creation knows all about the mistakes of His created and how to deal with them.

Let's capture the significant facts about that man's experience:

1. He *talked* himself into trouble.

2. What he *believed* he *received*—dogs.

3. What he *feared* came upon him—dogs.

4. By his *desire*, his *words*, his *belief*, he was delivered out of his trouble.

The Power of the Word has no sense of humor and does not recognize incongruous situations any more than does the power of electricity or of gravity.

There are dangers all around us due to the thoughts, fears, words, deeds of the undeveloped and the willfully evil thoughts of other human beings, and also the actions of lower animals. But these will never bother us unless we literally ask for trouble. By the power of our word we can, and sometimes unknowingly do, draw certain kinds of people and animals into our orbit of experience, and incite them to attack and greatly harm us. But we can learn how to use our power to avoid that and all other dangers. Any time we are frightened, or face a grave situation or problem, we can say: *"God is in this place,"* and invoke the very Presence of the Spirit for our aid and protection.

There are many forms of decree. We have just seen that fear is a form of saying "Let there be!" as Job so painfully discovered. The Bible tells us that picturing is also a powerful form of saying "Let there be." This is a form Solomon knew and used successfully. We use it, too, and often to our great harm, until we learn this part of our power and how to use it consciously for progressive good. Here is an example:

A woman who came for help said, "Why did my children turn out so badly when I tried so hard for them?" meaning they were poor, sickly, unhappy, beset by many problems.

But as our conference got under way, the reason stood revealed. She said:

"From the time my first child was born [she was a gray-haired woman, mother of five, grandmother of four], I used to think and plan what I would do if I were left alone, a widow. As the children came along I continued with my plans about how I would manage life and get along and raise my children if I were left alone, a widow. I used to tell my children not to be extravagant, not to waste anything, because if Dad should die we would make use of that. I even made them save useless things—string, paper grocery bags, leftover clothing, just about everything. I used to see myself going through the motions, carrying out the plans, of what I would do if I were left alone."

She *was* left alone, a widow, with five very young children to bring up.

"My husband died just after the time I had my plans

18

all complete. I knew everything I would do. Through the years since, I have done just about that. Do you suppose God was just waiting until I got everything in order before He took my husband?" she asked.

She had actually used the power to picture with words in an almost unbroken, steady stream. But she had used it to picture what she feared and most certainly did not want. *Fear is a form of consent.* It is faith in reverse. She had long been a church member, a Bible reader, but had never taken seriously, or had failed to understand, the law that says "Death and life are in the power of the tongue." Also, "As he [man] thinketh in his heart so *is* he," and so does he eventually become. She had spent many hours awake at night, in bed, thinking about being left alone, a widow, while her husband slept beside her.

Did her thoughts enter his thoughts and influence him? Both science and religion say yes.

That woman began, then, to learn about the spiritual laws and how to work with them. She started to study Truth as Jesus taught it, divorced from sect and creed, and to try to learn how to use the power of her word. Later, she said to me: "Now I see that I harmed my children by always talking about poverty and expecting bad times. But it is not too late to help my grandchildren."

Much later, the same woman said: "I see that I talked my poor, unsuspecting husband to death! What I should have done all those years was to think about, talk about, and picture all the wonderful things we would do together as we grew older. Instead, I kept him worried all the time about my own fears of being left alone with the children to bring up."

Latest of all she saw me and said: "The trouble was, I was not thinking about my husband's highest good. I was selfish, utterly, almost inhumanly selfish, and did not even recognize the fact. I thought only of what might happen to *me*! He did not know how to protect himself from my thought. I see, now, that I was a powerful broadcaster."

Every thought is a step in a journey toward what we want or do not want. We must learn to use our power of picturing to draw and keep ever bright the good, the true, the beautiful, the unlimited and lovely things and conditions that we do want in our life and in the lives of our loved ones. Here are some examples of how others have been helped to remember the power of their word:

A man who studied with me had trouble in watching his thoughts and words, even after he got his desires right. He liked to hunt and, in season, went up to the Mojave desert country to hunt for quail and rabbits. One day during our lesson together I said to him:

"Bill, have you ever thought about the tragedy of so many people being killed by 'unloaded' guns?"

"Yes, I have," he replied. "And the double tragedy is that so many of those fatal accidents have happened to children and by children."

"Remember," I said, *"every word you speak is loaded."*

He thought it through for a while in silence, then said: "That ought to teach me. I learned long ago how to handle a gun carefully. I always go on the premise that the gun is loaded and I keep all guns out of the hands of children."

"There is a further point," I said, "which might also help you. A gun can kill a man needlessly as easily as it can kill quail or rabbits that might be needed for food. So *learn to use your loaded words for a definite purpose!"*

It is a truth, dear reader; believe me, man is the freest thing on earth. Free to use his power to kill himself, or to grow to heights of which we do not now dream. What a pity so few know even the power of their ordinary, everyday spoken words, to say nothing of the collective Power of the Word, their Self or divine Being. All around me I see those spiritual infants who are actually talking themselves and others to death. Stop and listen in any group, and you will hear people talking about what they do not want in their lives or the lives of their loved ones. But the law says they will be both condemned and justified by their words.

How can we always be sure we are using the power of our word in the right way? We will take it up fully in our next chapter. Just now, let us catch up quickly on what we have learned and, at the same time, define some of our terms already used and point up others. They are listed here in this way so that the student may turn back to them from time to time as he goes on with his studies.

1. *Word of God*: You and I and all other human beings are each an individual Word of God.

2. *Power of the Word*: By virtue of being a Word of God (also termed Son of God), made in His image and likeness, we have some of the nature of our Creator. God created by the process of desire and decree. We too have the power to create by saying "Let there be!"

3. *Nature of the Power of the Word*: It is creative. It can create anew or assemble that which has already been created. It can create new cells in our human body and bring strangers together from the four corners of the earth. Or bring up memories of the past into the conscious mind. It can bring ideas from the Mind of God to anyone who learns how to ask for them and how to recognize them when they come. This fact science now states, as does religion. Edison and Steinmetz and other great persons, creators in many fields, knew and used this fact. So do modern engineers and designers, in aircraft and industrial plants of all kinds, use these facts today.

4. *Place of the Power of the Word*: The Power

itself resides in God or His set law, His will. But man's use of it was established for him and in him "from the foundation of the world." It has been delegated to man under spiritual law much as authority is delegated to an individual by power of attorney in man-made law. Hence, the delegated power or right and ability to use the Power of God resides in man, in each individual human being. Jesus made it clear that He of Himself did nothing, that instead it was the "Father within" who did the mighty works. All men have access to God through their individual "Father within," who is God, or all there is. Both the Old and the New Testaments establish this term *Father*, which Jesus used and we know as the Word, or the Son of God. Hence Jesus says, "No man comes to the Father [meaning God, the Creator] but by me"—except through the Son, meaning that Self which God created and empowered.

5. *How we set the power into motion:* By speaking the word, either with full intent and purpose or with "idle words." There are many forms of decree. Fear, silence which gives consent, love, cursing, and blessing are all forms of using the word.

6. *How the Power works:* No one knows. We can only observe that it does work. We must never try to tell the Power how to get what we want. We must know exactly what we do desire and speak the word for it.

7. *Speaking from the heart:* Our heart is the sum total of all we believe about all life, including our belief about God. We must therefore be careful of what we take into our heart, accept, believe. For we always speak both our idle words and those of purpose from our heart level.

8. *Mouth:* The Bible tells us repeatedly that the Power of the Word is ours to use, that it is in our very mouth.

9. *Power*, upper and lower case; *Word*, upper and lower case; and *Key*, we have already discussed.

10. *Objective:* The great objective of our life should be to raise the collective level of our heart. When this occurs for the individual, we have a better person. When it has happened for enough individuals, we will have a better world for all men.

11. *Decree:* The word means, says Webster: "An authoritative order or decision; edict; law; ordinance. To command authoritatively." It is just that. By our decree we determine what is to be done. The Power does the work, but we must speak the word, tell the Power what we want done. "The burden is every man's own word" (Jeremiah 23:36) is a fact we all should remember. But the word can also be wings for us. Jesus said that His burden was light. He knew how to speak the word correctly.

12. *Power:* Webster says power means "The ability, whether physical, mental, or moral, to act, the faculty of doing or performing something; capacity for action or performance, or for receiving external action or force." And further: "Control; authority; . . . influence . . . exerted . . . energy; vigor; force." And, under law, power means, "Capacity or right," especially delegated as "authority . . . as power of attorney."

All this is inherent in our thoughts, in everyday spoken words!

It amounts to a tremendous truth that is revolutionizing the entire lives of those individuals who learn about it and then begin to use the truth they learn. Even the Communists will learn the truth eventually and it will save them from themselves. For the truth is this:

God has given us the physical, mental, and moral power and right over our own lives, souls, and affairs.

Yes, even the Communists could learn the truth— that they have a power within themselves, within their own words, with which to "break the chains that bind them."

Our outer world is made according to our inner directions. Hence Jesus said, "The kingdom of God is in the midst of you." All the parables of Jesus were case histories of right or wrong use of the power of the word of an individual. Tomorrow's scientifically taught people will not be "anxious" for their days. Instead they will take well-considered and aimed thought for definite purposes and not be anxious about anything, for anxiety is a troublemaker and, as our modern doctors tell us, can be and often is a killer.

With all that power at our disposal, why do we so often get into trouble and lead such miserable lives of want and sickness? *Because we have free will.* We use the power against ourselves. We must learn to use the spiritual laws of the universe rightly, or constantly get into trouble by using our power of attorney in the wrong way. If we do not know the laws, obviously we shall act contrary to them. Just as obviously, we shall never take advantage of the riches of God that are at hand, awaiting our spoken decree, our use of them.

Having such power implies responsibility equal to the power. For every privilege carries responsibility. When we license an individual to operate a high-powered automobile, we place a responsibility for which he is held accountable along with his privilege. We would have a world of chaos otherwise. *The responsibility we face in using the Power of our Word is that of choice.*

What are we to do? We are using words all day long, all our life long. There are death and life in the power of the words we use. What are we to do? *Learn how to choose and use that which is good.* Learn how to do it consciously, time after time, with purpose afore-thought, or suffer the consequences. How?

Use Your Word for Creative and Progressive Good

If you continue in my word, you are truly my disciples, and you will know the truth, and the truth will make you free (John 8:31, 32).

In our first chapter we learned about the existence, nature, authority, place, and Power of our Word. Its nature is so highly creative that "Death and life are in the power of the tongue." Every time we speak, we turn on the Power in our Word or Self, which is God's power honoring our human spoken decree.

Our objective is to create good and ever more good for ourselves and others and to harm no one as we go through life, while promoting our soul growth. This is the way we best serve God. When we serve God, we are also serving our fellow men and ourselves.

Now we are ready to learn how to be sure we are using our word for *creative and progressive* good every time we set it into motion by any one of our many forms of decree.

Our first question is, what is good? The answer is, anything that cooperates with the purpose of life.

The purpose of our human life on earth is to grow. We grow by learning and doing. We must learn about and work with our three-level self and our three-level world.

We have dominion over all the world and we are to "dress and subdue" it and to perfect ourself. So we must learn about our physical, material, mental, and spiritual self and our world. The higher we go in the scale of intelligence, the more eager we are to learn the whole story of man, the who, what, why, when, where, and how of his existence. Science and philosophy give us many answers. But for the final why, we must look to religion.

Now we can state our rule:

Good is anything that takes us forward in our search for God and the answer of the eternal destiny of man. Evil is anything that holds us back. We can be taken forward or held back by desires, emotions, thoughts, words, acts—every form of decree.

We can be sure our words are creating good, our decrees taking us toward God, by seeing that our word is within the law of *love*, that it is *unlimited* (which presupposes the highest order of faith), that it is *specific* and *in order.* If we do this, we shall not have to worry about building our heart ever higher and higher. The progressive part of the problem will take care of itself.

We shall be learning this point throughout the rest of the book, but we can profitably start here by seeing the value of frequently checking up on ourself, asking, "Am I starting a vicious circle or a benevolent one?"

Vicious circles are often started by idle words. But they count. "On the day of judgment men will render account for every careless word they utter," said Jesus (Matthew 12:36).

Benevolent circles are started either from a heart of love and wisdom, or from careful attention and purpose.

Examples:

"Times are bound to get harder, thousands will be laid off from work, and thousands of factories closed."

The man who said that was speaking from a heart of fear and doubt. He was limiting God, fellow man, self. In using these words he was not describing what he wanted. They were idle words. They started a vicious circle that brought him almost to bankruptcy and a closed factory. He accepted the idea from someone else, believed it, talked constantly about it. Then he believed more and more as he spoke.

"God is unlimited and man is His child and therefore unlimited. As one job is finished, another will be begun as long as the world lasts. God has plans for man not yet dreamed of. New work and wonders beyond our present understanding are awaiting our awareness, our desires, and our asking. We can grow just as fast as we are willing to try to learn and do."

Those words, spoken by the same man, started a *benevolent circle.* He spoke them from a heart filled with faith, which unlimited God, himself, and his fellow man. He said what he had come to believe. He believed what he continued to say. The more often he said it, the more strongly he believed it. The more he believed it, the more he acted upon his belief. It is a law of nature.

We are always creating circles with our words, which start with the heart at its present level, go out into the world around us by their own power, come back to us as events, things, further ideas, and words that build our heart with love and limitlessness or fill it with fears, hatreds, unhappiness, and limitation.

Points to remember in building our heart and using our word for creative and progressive good:

1. *Love God, all good.*

Example: A man had met with many accidents, one after another. His wife came to me, wanting to know why he had suffered so much bad luck. She had been injured in an automobile accident with him and had made up her mind she would no longer subject herself to "these terrible things that are always happening to Ed."

Conferences with both of them revealed that the man was so filled with secret, silent hatred he was un-

27

consciously trying to destroy himself and others. He saw nothing good or beautiful in life, in other people, or in himself. He was a child of hate. When I told him he was asking for all the trouble he received, he at first refused to accept it as fact. But his wife was going to leave him unless "things were changed" and he knew it. Their five years of marriage had been one long-drawn-out series of unfortunate happenings. It took a long time but Ed did improve, finally came to love good so much that he joined a church, served in it, learned more good, and righted his life. His affairs changed as he learned. He came to see for himself that "God does exist and God is good," and to feel grateful for the peace and sense of security that knowledge gave him. His wife had a great deal to learn, too. She had to start with questions: "Why did I fall in love with a man like that? What drew him into my orbit?" She was not blameless either. None of us is.

2. *Understand something of the nature of God.*

The more we know about the nature of God and of man's relation to Him, the more our hearts will grow and be filled with all good. With the Bible, hundreds of good books and magazines, and hundreds of other means of learning, there is no excuse for anyone today not knowing about God. Besides all that, there are the weekly reports of modern science and industry which offer some of the most convincing arguments and proofs of Bible truths. The tragedy of it is that those who need most to know are those most unwilling to learn. It is so easy to get settled in a rut, where we stay until some great problem or desire lifts us out, or some tragedy blasts us out. All growth starts with desire.

3. *Depend upon God.*

A man whose real problem was that of indecision and plain laziness always blamed others for his failures.

He said he didn't take the job that had been found for him because it just didn't seem to him that it was "the will of God for him to work in that place." I asked him if he thought it was the will of God for his wife and young children to go hungry and poorly clothed. He shrugged and said, "If it is the will of God, they will be provided for."

He was both justified and condemned by his word. The welfare agencies (which exist because of the love in the hearts of people, and all love is of God) took care of his family. But the damage he had done his family and himself by saying and believing they were less than others could hardly be calculated. The stigma of "charity" may drive those children to acts of delinquency in their anger and need for hitting back at a foe they do not see or understand, but which has harmed them greatly. Society may have to pay their crime bills the rest of their lives. For in this case I have had opportunity to watch results of their hurt and anger while they are still quite young.

I cite the above case because so many people seem to be confused on the point of what is and is not the will of God. Students who are learning to use their word have hesitated and asked, "But how do I know it is right for me to ask for this [the good they desire, or the work they want to do] unless I first know whether or not it is the will of God?" They are overlooking the fact that they have free will, responsibility for using it, that "it is your Father's good pleasure to give," and that God wins when we accept the riches of His kingdom.

The will of God is nature, the sum total of all the spiritual laws. When we learn this truth, we shall be free from human bondage. We learn truth from our Bible, science, our own heart, and our daily observations. The will of God is not something that changes momentarily. It is not dependent upon caprice, mood, willfulness of the moment, or sacrifices of the petitioner. Many people suffer all their life long because they think the will of God is subject to change without notice. To one man I said:

"You seem to think God is not as dependable as an airplane or railroad train schedule." It changed his point of view.

If God worked as many think He does, we could not have a stabilized universe. Maybe we would have the light of the sun and it would stay in its orbit every day, or maybe God would be off the job some morning and forget to start things rolling and we would be frozen into nothingness. How ridiculous can we get? Everything that science discovers, whether in the atom or in the farthest star, proves that all is law and order and is *dependable.* Everything that religion discovers proves that all is *love.* Science is also coming to the point of love. There is a growing literature in science on this one subject alone. Browning, poet and therefore true seer, saw both points of truth and said, "All's love, yet all's law."

We can sum it up: We can depend upon God's love and law.

4. *Unlimit God in every way.*

Since we want to create progressive good, we must get our hearts filled with ideas that unlimit God. We must not tell God what to do or how to do it. Instead, only ask for what we want. Example:

An attorney needed some information in order to help him win a case for his innocent client. He had been speaking the word for information but it had not come. When we went into the matter, we discovered that he had been thinking God would have to find a certain man and through him produce papers that contained the desired information. That was the wrong way. It was saying there was only one way to do that job. But we must not limit "the Holy One of Israel." We cannot bring God and His ways down into our finite minds and ways. I told the attorney to unlimit God and to speak the word. He had forgotten the fact that he had only to convince himself that the Power could and would solve the problem. He did not have to convince himself *how* it would do this.

The attorney saw his mistake and stated it in legal phraseology which I could not follow. But he did unlimit God in his heart, mind, and word. He then spoke the word and cast the burden. He called it "resting the case."

Help came to him in time. But not through the man or papers the attorney had been asking for. His word accomplished when he unlimited God and himself.

Help will come to anyone who is trying to better his life by daily practicing unlimiting God. Think about the wonderful things that could be done to make life easier for all men. *Think in terms of miracles.* Make big plans for today and tomorrow. When problems arise that need expert handling say, "God can do it." Then, "If God can do it, He can tell me how to do it, too!" Then *listen.* That is a method used in a modern plant where they work with electronics. "We sit around and talk about God and wonder how He would do it, then we wait and listen," said a man who is a "lead man" in the plant. Unlimiting God means unlimiting yourself, also. Keeping in touch with the latest developments in science and the latest achievements of religion will help you to unlimit God and yourself as well as your fellow men.

5. *Love and unlimit all men.*

Make the Golden Rule your daily rule. It is a positive guide to keeping check on your words, thoughts, and deeds. It is the best human relations rule ever devised. Speak no word of limitation to others or against them. Stop all forms of domination, even in thought—because your thought reaches them and does its work against them, unless they know how to protect themselves. What you sow, you also reap. That is why you cannot afford to forget the "Do unto others as you would have others do unto you" rule. What goes out from you comes back to you.

Do not be ashamed or worried because you are not able to do mighty works with your word. The needful thing is to be headed right, learning. One of the best ways to have good ideas come to you is to appreciate those of other persons. It lifts you to a higher mental standing. You travel on a higher wave length.

Practice sending your fearless and encouraging thoughts to others, trying to be grateful for the work others are doing. Your good thoughts sent out will be duly picked up by those in tune with them. Often a great man (generic—throughout this book *man* means both men and women) working alone on some difficult problem finds his faith wavering. He rests, relaxes in a form of listening. As he does so, he tunes in to the thoughts of others on his spiritual level who, through their ministry of thought unlimited and love active, send him what he needs. I am sure no man succeeds alone. And the greatest men have always seemed to be a little astonished at their own accomplishments. So broadcast your thoughts and convictions of courage, gratitude, good will. Attending lectures, reading good books, going to church all help lift the consciousness level of all men. Every time you think and speak seriously about the power of God, the love of God, and the utter security of all men everywhere, you set benevolent waves into motion that others can pick up and use. The good eventually finds its way back to you.

6. *Love and unlimit yourself.*
Remember who you are: a child of God.
Remember what you are: a Word of God.

32

Remember your purpose of life on earth: to grow.

No one knows how much a man can do. If we are to use our word for more and yet more of livingness, we must never limit ourself in thought or belief about our own potentialities. No one has done all he is capable of doing. Each new achievement opens up new units of power. Any degree of self-pity or self-hate is limiting and destructive. It is walking toward death.

Example:

A woman who had made some very human mistakes was having trouble adjusting her life and affairs after she came out of jail. A welfare worker sent her to me. I told her she had to believe that God had forgiven her, that society had accepted her jail term and fine as payment of her debt to her fellow men, that it remained only for her to stop punishing herself. She was putting herself into a prison of her own thoughts.

"But there must be something basically wrong, terribly wrong with me," she sobbed. "I'll never live long enough to forget it, or to get over it."

"Those are words of fear and self-destruction," I warned her. "You are starting a new, vicious circle. Are you more moral than God? Well, then, since God has forgiven you, how foolish, how arrogant, how sinful not to forgive yourself! Since God loves you, your self-hatred is criticism of God's judgment and morals. Your duty is to grow, not to destroy yourself."

Shame persisted, so I tried a line of reasoning with her that has helped many with self-hatred and shame problems. I said:

"Once you were a baby, weren't you? And as a baby, you often wet your diapers, didn't you? Well, then, should you blush and cringe and cry today because of something you did quite naturally as an unknowing infant? Of course not. How silly that would be! It is just as silly to be so filled with shame and spiritual self-criticism for something you have done as an unknowing spiritual infant. In the sight of God you have made an unknowing spiritual-infant mistake. To you it seemed right at the time. Now you know better. Now do better. You have had a change of heart. *Speak a good word for yourself.* Because as you go out into the world thinking about yourself, others are going to think of you."

She learned to say:

"I love God and God loves me,

And I a better person will be."

She continued with her studies, righted her life, and was soon making a good contribution to the world.

Always love and unlimit yourself, today, tomorrow, and forever. Your desires at base came from God. You will naturally often make mistakes in trying to fulfill them. Especially until you learn the spiritual laws. But without trying there is no learning, and to learn is our objective on earth. Forgive yourself, love yourself, and go right on trying.

7. *Be specific.*

Example: There was a man who said he had failed all his life, but he was tired of being supported by relatives and of getting and losing jobs. He wanted me to speak the word for him. I said, "What are you going to ask for?"

"Just to kind of get along," he replied.

"But you have been doing that," I pointed out. "If you really want to speak the word, you must be able to name your desire. You must know exactly what it is you want to do. What jobs have given you the greatest pleasure? What work have you liked best of all?"

"Gardening," he promptly replied.

Then we knew exactly what to speak the word for, and he did. He got a job in less than a week.

8. *Get your decrees to agree.*

If we desire one thing, ask for another, and talk

about and believe in yet another, we get chaos and not our heart's desire. Example:

A man who very much wanted financial success and worked hard for it began to be successful. But when friends complimented him, he would pretend it was a mere nothing. "Not much," he would say, playing himself down. "I'm not so smart." He began to have business reverses until he learned to make his decrees agree. For order is heaven's first law. There can be no harmony of life and affairs without order. *Say what you mean and mean what you say* is the rule.

9. *Rule your Spirit.*

Keep a tight rein on your intents, purposes, desires, to see that they are all under the law of love and without limit. It is easier to take a city, as the Bible intimates, than it is to rule our own spirit. A professional dog trainer told me his job "is a cinch compared to making myself do the right thing at the right time." One of the points we must closely watch is impatience. Example:

"Why doesn't God come right out and tell me what I want to know?" a woman asked me angrily.

"Some have ears and hear not," I reminded her. "God *is* telling you. You say things to your young baby that he does not understand, even though he hears every word you say. We are all spiritual infants of different ages, children of God, and as yet we know very little. Be patient in your learning and doing. Impatience is a sign of both fear and distrust. If you will become quiet enough in spirit, you will hear the voice of God telling you what to do. *Learn to listen.*"

10. *When in doubt...*

When in doubt about the desire of your heart for which you are going to speak the word, ask yourself: "Why do I want this? What do I expect it to help me to become?'' Nearly all our desires are for things which we hope will help us become something. We ask for things which we believe will give us more courage or happiness or some other feeling. That is inverting the power. We should ask to *become* a happy person, to *become* a better person or successful or well or whatever it may be. And then follow it up with our part—speaking, thinking, doing in kind with our desire.

Thus we complete our benevolent circle. Speaking from our heart into the world, it comes back to our heart again, building up or tearing down. Our objective always is to build more love, more faith, more daring to do, more gratitude for being, more and ever more unlimited. To do this day after day is to lead a good life and obtain the desires of our heart. But most important of all, it is to grow surely and safely toward God.

When people begin to do practical things in life by learning how to use the power of their own individual word, they are nearly always astonished at their previous lack of knowledge and interest. A woman who had just acquired a new home through asking for it, said:

''Isn't it strange that we wouldn't think of buying a home without knowing all about the electric wiring in the house, number and location of the outlets, and whether we could use our electric equipment and appliances there, but we go all through life without ever thinking of our own potential power within ourself with which we are wired, or how to use it!''

No, it is not strange. It is natural unfoldment. We are all working toward the higher development which is necessary for us to become co-workers with God. Here and there are people who have learned enough about the power to use it deliberately for solutions to their problems and for steps in soul growth. The number is daily increasing.

Successful people who know how to use their word

appear to lead a charmed life. Those in ignorance of the power sometimes resent and envy the "good luck" of the knowing users. Such people may covet the possessions of the happy and successful ones, never realizing they could do as much or more for themselves through learning how to ask for it, employing the power God gave them.

Probable questions with answers:

1. What is the difference between prayer and speaking the word?

Answer: Prayers of petition are made to God asking His help. Speaking the word is using the power that God has given us, which will be honored. We speak directly to the thing or condition. Jesus cursed the fig tree directly. He spoke the word directly to the man with the palsy. Yet Jesus spent whole hours in prayer. Prayer increases our faith and knowledge so that we use our word directly without hesitation, setting it into motion.

2. Is there a pattern or formula to be used in the practice of speaking the word?

Answer: Yes. We take it up in chapter four and use it from there on. These earlier chapters are to get our principles straight.

The Mental
and Spiritual Powers of Man

*He who believes in me will also do the works that I
do; and greater works than these will he do* (Jesus
in John 14:12).

*The word is near you, on your lips and in your
heart* (Romans 10:8).

*It is not you who speak, but the Spirit of your
Father speaking through you* (Matthew 10:20).

In the previous chapter we learned that we can be
sure we are using our word for creative and progressive
good by seeing that it comes within the *law of love*, is
unlimited (which presupposes the highest kind of confidence or faith), is *definite* (which means specific and
in *order*). That is the way we speak a creative and good
word and so build our heart that succeeding words will
prove progressively good.

Now the question arises: What is the scope of our
power of decree? How much authority do we really
have and on how many planes of intelligence and life?
Why do we have this power and what is the ultimate use
we are to make of it? If we can get answers to these
questions, we shall find use for them every hour of our
life, for they will give meaning to all life.

To seek the answers is to find ourself in very good
company. Today many of the world's wisest and best
people are asking these questions and trying to get convincing and provable answers to them. Many are
receiving answers that satisfy, amaze, delight, and

humble them, stimulating them to further private research.

There are many organizations which exist solely for getting answers to questions concerning religious beliefs. All over the world Christians have long asked: "Can we get answers to our religious questions as material science gets answers to its questions? Can we prove that God exists? That prayers are answered? That there is survival after death? *Can we learn to do the things Jesus did?*"

In 1948 a small group of New England ministers started an organization to try to get answers. Their questions grew into the Religious Research Foundation which was later incorporated in the state of Massachusetts.

That organization, through its director, Reverend Franklin Loehr, head of the Los Angeles branch of the foundation, released records of their first scientific experiments with prayer. What they reported may eventually prove to be the forerunner of the best news on earth since the advent of Jesus Christ. They are going on with their work to try to establish other points of religious beliefs now held only on faith.

Using strictly scientific methods, the foundation worked with seeds and ivy plants. Since the story with photographs and charts has been published throughout the country, we need here mention only the points which have to do with the purpose of this book, the lessons we shall be studying together.

1. The researchers proved that seed germination and plant growth can be promoted by the means of prayer.

2. They proved that seeds and plants can be made to wither and die by means of negating them.

Two identical plantings of seeds were made. All conditions throughout were the same except that they directed *prayer* to one planting and the other was *negated.* Some twenty-one thousand seeds were used and eighty thousand measurements taken. Photographs and charts showed how the plantings *aided by prayer* flourished, while the *negated* plantings *withered and died.* Those doing the measuring and photographing did not know which plants were being prayed for, which were being negated.

"If you can cripple a plant in two minutes by negative thinking, as we have done, may we not also be crippling ourselves with negative thinking?" asked the modest and cautious Dr. Loehr in speaking of the experiments.

I have long known and admired Franklin Loehr and have worked with him on prayer projects. As a minister his enthusiasm about the findings of the foundation is boundless. As a scientist he leans over backward in being cautious as, of course, he should. Loehr was by profession a research chemist. He became chaplain in World War II, and after the war he entered the ministry. If we look at his scientific statement and for the time being ignore his caution, we find a startling fact which may yet hit the world with a greater impact than atomic bombs. He said,

"If we can cripple a plant in two minutes by negative thinking, as we have done, may we not also—"

May we not also, we should all arise and ask, *wither a fig tree as Jesus did?*

The Bible does not call the process negative thinking or negating a thing. It calls it cursing. That is what I call it, too. Webster defines *curse* as "to call upon divine or supernatural power to send injury upon." Webster says *negate* means "to deny, contradict or refute; to prove nonexistent."

The foundation experimenters could not deny that the ivy plants or the planted seeds existed. They could not contradict or refute the life and the laws in the seeds and plants. That is out of the jurisdiction of man.

40

But they could and they did use the *power of their word*, a power that God has given to every man. The time has come when Christians everywhere must realize this fact and put it to use. For either we have to believe that Jesus meant what He said when He said that man could learn to do what He did "and greater," or we have to say that there is nothing to the Christian beliefs and philosophy.

Consider the foundation's report once again:

Besides ivy plants, grains were planted, and the prayed-for ones sprouted and grew. The negated grains either did not sprout at all or were deficient; some were actually blasted, then dried up and died. Some of the plants were "crippled in two minutes." All this was done through the intent, purpose, and *power of the word of a group of people.*

"You will decide on a matter and it will be established for you, and light will shine on your ways" (Job 22:28).

Light, throughout the Bible, indicates spiritual and mental powers, ability to know and do. Does this not mean the same thing Jesus meant when He stated it in other words? Jesus indicated that a man might light his own pathway from light within himself.

"Death and life are in the power of the tongue" (Proverbs 18:21) is not just a figure of speech. It describes a principle of life.

A new day is dawning in which life on earth will be better for all men than it ever has been for any man to date. It is being born of the union of science and religion, which will free man from bondage of earth by showing him the powers he has *within himself.* A new world of abundance and freedom for the individual beyond our former wildest dreams is now possible through the tremendous increase in the knowledge of man himself. Soon all the peoples of earth will have the opportunity to walk on two feet—faith and fact. Then

41

the human race will climb to heights of doing, being, and having such as we cannot now imagine.

But the individual need not wait for that sunrise which will awaken and quicken the whole human race. The individual is as unlimited as he thinks he is. No one can stop him in his mountain climbing but himself. Helping people with their problems has given me contact with many wonderful and some quite unusual and far-advanced students of life. They generously share with me what they have experienced in their own lives, what they think, believe, and dream about the possibilities of the powers within man. I ask them to write down these facts and views and give them to the world. But none has yet done so. Nor have they given me permission to quote them. Their excuse is, "People would not believe it," or "People would call me crazy," regarding the things some of them have accomplished. One man, high in the world of affairs, said that he would doubtless be asked to resign from his high-paying job if his interest and experiments in a certain line of human powers were made public.

But we cannot leave it all to the experts, the professionals, the scientists, the great ministers and mystics, but must, as ordinary people in every walk of life, reveal our individual learnings and yearnings. For "the voice of the people is the voice of God," and thousands know absolute truths, facts about life, natural laws, and forces that they have not learned from books or other men. They have received their information directly from God, which the Bible claims anyone can and may do who prepares himself to receive. It is the way the prophets got their facts. We should have more prophets today than they had two or three thousand years ago. Today's science explains how it could happen. I believe it is happening and will continue to do so.

I think the human race is rapidly approaching the place where there will be many who have learned to listen and to tell what they have learned—modern prophets, if you will. In this atomic age it may well be that such individuals, who have the deep desire, the time and faith to listen, the patience to wait, the persistence to try and try and try, will point the way out of our seeming present confusion, rather than the politicians and the professional better-world planners.

It is my hope that the reader will join the ever-growing number of individuals who not only accept as fact that man can learn to do the things Jesus did, but will go quietly and calmly about the business of taking the first steps toward such learning and doing.

Where should you start? Right where you stand. Use what you have to get more of anything you want. The laws of life say that before we can do or have, we must first *be.* Our question, then, is how to become more? By exercising the powers we have, by starting where we are. In a desire to help I will give here some experiences of trying to grow, from my own life, and ask the reader to excuse my becoming personal.

Some years ago I wrote an article that was published in Clear Horizons magazine, in which I suggested that groups of people of very high faith get together and create pools of faith into which sufferers could go with prayers and be healed. Since faith is the key to successful use of the power of prayer, we should help each other by pooling our faith. Later, I found just such a pool of faith in a small church not far from my home. I have attended Sunday morning services there nearly every Sunday since then, working with the power of the word as best I can.

I here report the circumstances, because the results of my trying to *speak the word* for others while in that church have been most heartening. I have received confirmation of healings of many kinds taking place during the time of the service or shortly after, and of some that have taken place a number of months later, during which time I had continued to work on that same problem. Any individual can start a pool of faith in his own church.

1. The church I speak of is small. They have only about two hundred and fifty members. It was conceived in prayer and is the most spiritual of any church I have ever known. People I have invited there say on first attendance, "There is something different going on here." Some have been healed just by attending the Sunday morning services. The members are not eager to increase membership too quickly, for they see that entrance of many of lower or little faith might damage their pool. I agree.

2. The church observes the rule of silence. The members of the congregation feel that the "Lord is in His holy temple," and that the least they can do is to keep silent. There is a fifteen-minute meditation period to soft organ music before the service begins. It is at this time of silence and music, the church filled, that I take up one person at a time on my treating list and *speak the word* for him. Also, to each, silently, just as if I were in his presence.

Is silence conducive to soul growth and faith building that enable one to speak the word effectively? I think so. Jesus went into the desert to get away from crowds and seems to have spent all night alone in prayer at intervals. Was He getting away from their physical presence only, or from their thoughts, fears, jealousies, even hatreds that closed in on Him when there were too many of them, and so prevented Him from doing His work? Did Jesus have to go alone and cleanse His own spirit in a form of erasing the negative thoughts He had unavoidably accumulated from the crowds? And from the hate-fear thoughts others must have directed at Him? I think so. How much more so, then, do we need to bathe often in pools of faith!

Does music add to faith, help the soul grow, remind

the hearer of God's love, open the inner powers for receiving the Word of God, enable us to speak a more positive and powerful word for others? I think so. I think we have not yet started to scratch the surface of the possibilities of musical therapy. *The right kind of music.* Here is a field of research for individuals and small groups. It can be carried on in any church, in homes, in a private pool of faith. Music and dancing have always been associated with religious experiences. We must learn why.

3. The minister of that church is a woman who is very devout and spiritually developed. She is a fine balance of love and intellect. The church is her life. *She believes what she preaches.*

Good is to be had in any church, any time, anywhere. All are to be protected, respected, supported. They represent different levels of understanding and growth. But some churches have become vast organizations, with many committees, meetings, money-raising events until the spirit of church is lost, overrun by social actionists of one kind and another who seem to have given up contact with God and use the church as a voters' club to try to create better manmade laws. In such churches I feel the tensions, fears, worries, even hatreds and disturbances that I feel on city streets. I find it easier to pray effectively in my automobile, driving to and from such a church, than while I am there, a part of the congregation—a fact which continues to distress me deeply. I cannot even try to *speak the word* in churches of that kind.

Is not faith in the church one of its first duties? I think it is difficult, if not impossible, for one to be healed in a church where there is little faith. The Bible (Acts 5:15,16) tells how the faithful of the church brought their sick to be healed, which implies that the members of the church had a deep pool of faith. Again (Matthew 13:59), we find that Jesus "did not do many mighty works there, because of their unbelief." Does this not mean unbelief of the church members as well as of the individuals who needed to be healed? Here is a place for religious research that any individual can carry on, and organize a group to work with him.

It seems certain beyond doubt that, in a group of people gathered in prayer and meditation, people of an above-average spiritual level of belief, faith is multiplied. This is the pattern for Glenn Clark's famous Camps Farthest Out prayer groups that are making religious history. It is the method used by the Church of Religious Science, Unity, and others in the Truth or New Thought group. Many orthodox churches are using it, too. All the Christian world is turning back to the use of prayer for healing the sick.

4. The members of the small church mentioned love their work. As individuals they have high hopes of a better world tomorrow. And their hopes hinge not on things but on the spirit, the love, the heart of man. Their seeking is of the soul, to become better persons, to learn how to do the things Jesus did by becoming more and more Christlike.

When we go to my church, it seems to me that there is something in the very walls of the building, the boards of the floor, that is conducive to peace, healing, love, truth, goodness—to an insight into all life. At times there is a feeling that "something good and wonderful is about to happen, and when it does, all life on earth will ever after be the better for it." That is about as near as I can come to describing it.

The building itself seems to me to store up something which it radiates back again to the people who come in. I am not going too far in saying that healing currents of living faith are somehow generated there. I can feel them quite as definitely as I can feel a current of warm air. It makes the hair stand up on the back of my neck and sometimes raises "goose pimples" over my arms and over my whole body. There is always a high level of spirit there. But there are times when it climbs and climbs. It is a wonderful experience. It is during these "high" times that my word does "accomplish."

Do all surfaces radiate back into the surrounding area in homes, churches, cities, countries, the powerful vibrations of thoughts, words, feelings, desires that have been released there? Do we have the power to inject hate and fear into inanimate things? I think so.

From the growing examples of this seeming fact I submit only the following:

A certain house that was originally built with what were said to have been stolen funds and had a long history of spiritually illegal owners came to my attention and service. It was one of the most difficult and exhausting jobs I ever tackled, but before we were through we had put so much love into it that our problem was solved and also the problems of some of the tenants. They accepted the love and prayers at work for them. Not so the owners. They put the place up for sale and it was bought by yet another spiritual-lawbreaker type. Did the house draw such an owner once again? A whole new set of tragedies occurred with the new owner. Is there a scientific basis for folklore along this line, and for ghost stories? Was Jesus referring to this fact about nature when He told His apostles to shake the dust from off their feet when they went into a town that would not accept their teachings? Can we bless oil and water so that they will heal? I think so.

In a lecture I related the facts about the house to make a point of the importance of praying in church where there are good feelings and vibrations, where the petitioner can draw from the pool of faith. After the lecture a woman told me about her daughter, married to an American army officer who was stationed in Germany. She said:

"My daughter has never before been afraid of anything in her life. Neither has her husband. They are living in a house formerly occupied by Nazis. She writes that they are frightened all the time, and that they never go to bed without a gun beside them."

Can the thoughts of people—hatreds, fears, desires for revenge—ruin a whole nation, impoverish it, bring on wars? I think so. I think Jesus taught that truth throughout His whole ministry. This is what Herbert Hoover, former President of the United States, said:

"I returned in 1919 from several years abroad (including most of the years of World War I) steeped with two ideas: First, that through three hundred years America developed something in a way of life of a people, which transcended all others in history; second, that out of the boiling social and economic caldron of Europe, with its hates and fears, rose miasmic infections which might greatly harm or even destroy what seemed to me to be the hope of the world."

Mr. Hoover was a deeply religious man and did a great deal of thinking about spiritual laws. He was an engineer and had to have facts for his opinions. He was not likely to go off the deep end in anything. While listening to what he said, we might well remember that this nation was founded by people who wanted a place to worship God as they were led by the Spirit and saw fit to do.

5. The people of that little church love me. This must be mentioned if we are to consider any other part of the program I have been trying to carry out there (unknown to a single one of the persons in that church—if they read about it here, it will be the first they know of it), for the success of my *speaking the word* is due to their love. Jesus' command to love one another might well have deeper meaning than most of us attach to it. Fellowship is good, we all know. But is there not something more involved? I think so. Tracing

down the power of love in the Bible, we come face-to-face with the fact: God is love. Then if those people love me, I must surely get the benefit of their combined power, the units of God that they are, because of their love. Now we are back to the words of Jesus—that we can do things by speaking the words that are in our very own mouth because, after all, they are not just our human words, but those of the "Father within" us. It is God-power doing the work! Then anyone can do it who has the faith and tries to make of himself a channel through which God can work.

Anyone who has the faith—there is the crux of the matter. We are back to the points of our two earlier chapters: *We must build our heart. We can do more when we are more.*

We certainly have the power to build our own heart consciousness. Both religion and science tell us how. Prayers, affirmations, study, meditation, listening, church attendance and participation all play their part.

To continue to be personal, I take specific time daily for this work. And if I waken in the night, or too early in the morning, my sleep over, I use the silence for prayer, for renewing my faith in the principles of Truth, recalling instances of prayer answered, of Truth made manifest. In summer, or in good weather, I sometimes arise and go into my garden at four or earlier in the morning, before the disturbing vibrations of the community begin. I walk around and look at the morning stars and listen. There seems to me to be a great, living, loving presence brooding over the whole world that is mindful of all that goes on, everywhere on earth, with a kind of master tape recorder keeping tab of human activities, thoughts, desires, prayers, words, sensitive to the least pull of need for help from a human being, even the cry of a newborn babe.

Does such a Spirit exist? With all my heart I believe it does. I think this is the very Spirit that Jesus was talking about when He spoke of the "Holy Ghost" and the "Spirit of truth," and also the "Comforter" (in the Book of John). My experiences in working with others lead me to conclude that even the very sick and mentally disturbed as well as the young are aware of this Spirit and pick up truth and help that comforts them. I shall relate two instances in the chapter on habits.

In all the above, nothing is listed that the reader, anyone, could not also do. But many may be asking, as they often ask me in person and when I lecture in public: "But why should we try to learn now to do the things Jesus did? Why don't we just relax and let nature take its course? If we are destined to learn eventually, we shall learn."

The answer is, because now we have the atomic bomb and the hydrogen bomb and others more deadly in the making. We have shortened our own time.

If we can wither a plant, cripple a plant in two minutes, may we not also *move a mountain?*

Why should we be interested in moving a mountain? A mountain is a stockpile of atoms. The atom is one of God's building blocks. The cells in a plant or a grain of corn are composed of atoms. The question is, can a man, a group of men, with a large enough pool of faith command an atomic bomb *not to explode?* Science is right now interested in such questions. We ought to be thinking about them, too.

David Sarnoff, of the Radio Corporation of America, has said, "Every achievement on the physical plane packs danger as well as opportunity."

We can add that every achievement on the mental and spiritual plane also packs a danger, as witness mob psychology and propaganda through hate and fear. Jesus withered a fig tree. Plants have been withered by a power of the human word and will, not because human beings spoke it but because God honors His promises to man. Even when man is about to kill himself with his own powers? Yes. Otherwise, how come we by war, crime, and sin?

Where does all this leave us? Right where we have always been: love or perish. Man is so power-packed that his idle words create good or evil. There is only one safe, one sane, one pleasant, one profitable thing to do: learn the law of love and live it. What chaos might we not create without the law of love! But God is not mocked. We can go just about so far with our powers and then we run into the snag of no faith, and there the power gives out for us. Every thought, word, deed, desire contrary to the law of love lessens our faith.

What the world is really facing today is a contest between things of the spirit and things of the world— the physical, mechanical things. For unless the Spirit of love controls the things created by body and mind, mechanics, materials, then man might indeed blow up his earth home and make of it a dead planet on which nothing can survive. Science already tells us that we can do this, and many fear that we are already headed for doing just this.

Personally, I do not go along with those who view with alarm. I view with joy, hope, and thanksgiving. The world is not going to the dogs. It is going to God. We are headed for the greatest era on earth that has yet been, better than anything we can plan or dream of. And *we can help to bring it in.*

Let's accept this fact into our hearts forever and begin to work with it here and now: *We can learn to do the things Jesus did.*

Jesus made it clear that not He, the Son of man, the Being they gazed upon, ate with, walked with, talked with, did the mighty works, but an intelligent *force*, a power that He termed the "Father" did the works. He used the power of His word in a "loud voice" when He raised Lazarus from the dead. The point is that *his word was honored.* Things happened. They didn't happen

51

until Jesus *spoke the word* for them to happen. Jesus said our word would be honored, too, if only we could believe. Jesus didn't say we would have to become pure and holy, join a church, tithe our time and money, worship God, or even call Him good. We had to do only two things: *believe* and then come under *love*, so that we do not destroy ourself by using the power God has given us.

Why don't we believe? The trouble is that we know too much that isn't so and too little that is so. We are too sophisticated. We lack humility. We lack love. We fail to become as little children, to accept as little children, to look with the awe and wonder of little children. But that is the way we learn about the power God has given us. It takes an almost all-out abandonment of reason, a state of mind akin to that of the child's utter belief in Santa Claus or fairies, at the start of daily conscious use of our power. Hence Jesus tells us to become as little children. Emerson spoke of an almost "insane insight or belief." Some of my good fellow Methodists look at me a little alarmed when I talk this way. Privately they think I am a little insane. God bless them; I would that they were a little insane, afire with this great new age of faith and works that is opening up to man.

Believe as children. That is the way to start, letting out all the rope, all reservations, all if's, and's, and but's. Afterward, it develops into a very sobering experience. We begin to reason and to learn, to grow. The more we learn, the more our awe increases. We move up beside the Psalmist and ask along with him, as every scientist is doing today, what *is* man? When fact after fact piles up, and demonstration is made with a deliberate intent and use of the laws and the power of our word, we begin to see beyond any doubt that God is indeed mindful of man. This is a fact modern science is hourly proving even to the so-called nonbelievers.

There is a growing literature in this one field of science alone. Even the Communists are going to believe. For, though they are screaming denial, the fact remains, they are children of God.

What is man? He is a Word of God with the power of attorney to act as God would act under given circumstances, within the terms (laws) of this "unspeakable gift" of the Giver.

What can be God's purpose in having given so much power to man? Well, why did God create man in the first place? We do not need to bother ourself too greatly with these weighty questions. Certainly God has some plan for man. We cannot be of much help in the plan until we learn how to form good and avoid forming evil by using the power we have. And we know the power is there. Life and learning in every branch is an orderly process, a procession from the lower to the higher always, an unfolding of the within to the without. We are on earth to learn. The purpose of our power while on earth is not just to heal the sick, feed ourself, create comfort—good and important as these are.

The real reason for our power is to train us in the use of our free will, the *power to choose*. Perhaps nothing less than the tragedies that we bring upon ourself by wrong choice and use, and the joys and peace beyond understanding that we attain by a right use of choice, could ever train the mind of man and lead him to control his spirit—the field of intent and purpose.

What is God's final plan for man? Who can know? Perhaps we, too, must learn to say, "Let there be!" and create a planet. Or manage a star world, or other forms of God's creation. Perhaps we may be allowed to volunteer to play the Christ role to other peoples in yet other worlds. Who can tell? I believe that during the next twenty-five or fifty years we shall learn more about the spiritual and mental powers of man than man has learned in the last five thousand years. We shall learn it from science and religion, working together for the benefit and salvation of all mankind.

In the next chapter we start out trying to use what we have thus far learned. As we go into the examples and exercises from life, and the directives, we must ever keep in mind that our real goal, way out yonder in time, is to become co-workers with God. We must remember that all these everyday aids are for the worthy purpose of training, however simple the mechanics and symbols to remind us may be. Just now we are like babies who are trying to learn to stand, walk, and talk. Life offers us many stumbling blocks and falls. But we are learning how to walk and presently shall be headed toward— walking steadily with knowledge aforethought of—our great goal.

Make Your Words Profitable Servants

"Put me to the test, says the Lord *of hosts, if I will not open the windows of heaven for you and pour down for you an overflowing blessing"* (Malachi 3:10).

After three chapters of learning our principles, we are now ready to use what we have learned. Our truth is of small good to us unless it will enable us to solve our everyday problems here on earth, and to help us obtain our greatest hearts' desire. For by these activities we shall help our soul to grow, and only by becoming more can we become enough to work with God's plan for man.

Nearly everyone thinks that if only he had enough money, all his other problems would speedily be solved. It isn't true, but most people are so persuaded, and therefore we will take up the problems in that field first.

The same pattern or formula for speaking the word can be used for all other problems. Every part of it is based on spiritual laws. It has four parts:

1. *Name your desire.*
Reason: Until you can name it, you are not sure what you are asking for. Your word must be specific, definite. Example: "I want to increase my income."

2. *Draw and hold a picture of the desire answered.*
Reason: You provide a pattern for the power of your word to follow much as an architect prepares

plans that are made into blueprints and printed specifications which the contractor is to follow. And also, a blueprint which you, the owner, are to keep in possession and in mind, to help you avoid changing.

Example: See yourself using the increased income, owning, enjoying the things you want to buy, or the services, privileges, purposes for which you are asking the increase. Warning: thoughts, words, deeds, feelings must all be in line with your pictured finished desire.

3. *Speak the Word.*

Reason: The contractor cannot build your house, even with your plans and specifications in his hands, until you engage him to do so. Your spoken word sets the power into motion.

Example: "I am speaking the word for myself, John Jones (using your own name or the name of the one you desire to help), and I am asking the Infinite Spirit to go before me and do all that is necessary for me to receive the greatly increased income for which I ask. Let there be an increase in perfect ways and under grace. I ask it in the name of myself, and through the power that God has given me. I know that this is now being done for me even while I ask; for it is not I who do the work, but the Father within. Father, I thank Thee for this good and perfect work."

4. *Move toward your goal.*

Reason: If you do not take definite steps toward your goal you will, through daily influences, unconsciously move away from it, which means you will cancel your order.

Example: If a contractor were building a home for you and you went to the job every day and changed your mind, told him one day not to build, the next, to go ahead, he would become frustrated and give up. And probably sue you for damages, to boot.

How do you move toward your goal? By watching every thought, word, and feeling. This is where affirmations come in. There is no point in speaking the word for a definite, set purpose and then by words to the contrary, by fear, or by some other means, canceling it. How are we going to handle that? First, see that the purpose is to continue to *convince yourself* that the work is being done. Then, do all that you can to keep your conviction intact. This is exactly the point Jesus stressed: *Believe* you have already received and then you will receive.

Many in the New Thought movement have their own regular formulas for this part of speaking the word. It is a form of reasoning according to Truth. Those who have enough faith do not need it. But most of us need to work for faith daily and, when we speak the word for a specific purpose, to step up the faith as high as we can.

The following line of reasoning was used by one of my students who wanted to increase his business. It is given as an example, but the student should work out his own, according to his understanding.

"I, John Jones, am a child of God, and my mind is a center through which God-Mind works. God always works for fuller expression and growth. Therefore God will work through my mind for any good work I desire to do. I need not do this work alone, for God in me knows what to do and God in me will take me through to greater and greater growth. What blesses me blesses all. My success is God's success. All that needs to be done will be done. All that is required, whether ideas, persons, things, opportunities, or whatsoever is necessary for the expansion and growth of this business (naming it) is even now coming to me. For the law says that before I ask, the answer is given and, while I am yet speaking, I will be heard and my word honored. The law says that I will receive as I believe. I ask, believing. And so it is done, even now."

Rule: Continue to believe that the work is being done because you have already received. Your idea of the thing you want is the first form of that which you are to receive. You already have *received the idea.* Hence Jesus said to believe that you have received. It is this idea that "becomes flesh" and will *come to you.* It will help you to say: "God wanted me to have this good and so He gave me the idea first; He offered it to me, and I accepted it. I have already received. Now the power in my word will clothe it and all the world may then see it, too."

In working with students, I have found that to give them *pictures of principles* and simple rhymed jingles of great truths helped some of them more than all the "heavy brain work," as one student worded it, that they could do. So I tell them and I tell you, one of the most effective ways to remember the power of your word and to use it correctly is to *think of your ideas, which your words express, as people.*

Ideas are living things. Ideas are people. By your word you give them birth; you express and ejaculate them out into the world. The kind of words you use will clothe them, give them personality. Ideas must be thought of as a race of people or a form of human beings. They are Logos.

The next step is to *picture your idea people* as going out into the world as your servants, friends, representatives, and business agents, for any service that you require of them.

Make your picture of your idea people so vivid with *color, shape, form,* and *action* that they will stay in your memory. Then form the habit of often stopping in your daily life to picture your idea people at work, for they will work according to their kind.

You will be sending out strong, positive intelligent servants, friends, ambassadors of good will, to represent you and bring back to you according to their kind.

Or they will go out as surly, unhappy, weak, destructive servants, or as fools that confuse others and bring back failure to you. Remember, they will complete their circle and come back to you, into your life, as things, affairs, conditions, and into your heart as convictions, emotions, new desires, new beliefs, and new facts. Thus our phrase "Nothing succeeds like success" is a true one. The Bible says that those who have not (a high consciousness), even the little that they have (of consciousness and so, of worldly goods) will be taken from them and given to those who do have (a high consciousness and so, who continue to build their heart and therefore to receive more and more). If you have a poor consciousness, you will send out a population of poor ideas, little word people who are cold, ragged, and hungry.

Do you think all this is just childish nonsense? Well, try it out for yourself. Make this experiment, right now:

Hold the book down a little so that its pages are flat before you, like the surface of a landing field for airplanes. Now speak aloud the words: *All* that the Father has is mine. Again, aloud: All that the *Father has is mine*. This combination of words is a complete *idea*. Remember now, that an idea is an *entity*. It has *life*, *intelligence*, and *form*.

Finally: *All that the Father has is mine!* Say it with deep conviction and now, watch what happens.

As the words leave your mouth the *idea* they express, the little living being, lands on the pages of this book. He is bouncing a little and taking form before your very eyes. See, it is a little human being, perfectly formed, his head not much larger than the letter *o*. Watch him! He is growing rapidly. He is expanding all over. Now he is as large as he ever will be—one inch tall and perfectly formed so that you can plainly see all his features and his clothing in every detail. You can see and understand the expression in his face and in his eyes. He is a *living being*. He is *your word* made flesh, just as you are a Word of God made flesh. He is a living idea, as much as you are alive. And he will be like you, have the same powers you have but in a different form.

Watch him closely. He is springing up, off the page! He rises into the air and circles around several feet above the book to get his bearings, for he must go out and away to do your bidding. There, he has found the way. Up he goes! He nears the ceiling, becomes invisible, mingles with the light. Henceforth he travels on the invisible rays that fill all space.

Gone from your view on business for you.

No eye on earth can see him. No ear can hear him. No hand can touch him. He will never make himself known to taste or smell. But he will go unerringly about your business. He is as real as you are real. For he is alive. He is intelligent. He will gather together little entities like himself unto himself—other ideas, and mingle with them, go about building the structure you have ordered, the desire of your heart, according to what? According to those plans and specifications you have drawn up and are keeping in mind!

Will he, really? Yes, of course he will. He is one of your workers who knows how to go about his business as well as any living cell in your body knows how to go about its business. Better. For he is a much higher type of organization than the physical cells in your body. He is unlimited in space, speed, and time. The only limit to his accomplishments is that set by his nature, the nature *you* gave him.

Solomon knew and used the facts we are discussing here. He was the richest man in the world of his day. The Bible expressed it as "the birds of the air will carry your voice, or some winged creature tell the matter." Henry Ford also knew and used this law. He talked about the "little entities that go to and fro," that came to bring harm or help. But Ford seems not to have connected it with the fact that we ourself set those little entities loose. He saw them as free entities already in the world all around them and called them also "little souls." Both views are correct. That is why our word can collect others like itself and bring them back to us, for our use.

To the student who wants scientific proof of this process I suggest that he obtain a copy of "The Soul of the Universe," by Dr. Gustaf Strömberg and keep it for repeated reference.

Now let us see how it works out in life:

Back in 1932, all the world seemed to be broke after the 1929 financial crash. A businessman who long had used the principles found in the Bible (and which I have written about in my three previous books) took on a bankrupt business and made a fortune out of it. Years later he sold the business and retired. But the man who bought him out did not understand the principles which the first owner had used to build a business and a fortune. He was a very different type of man. In a few years the business was losing money. It reached a desperate stage and grew worse.

Several of the salesmen and other employees begged the former owner to do something to save the company and their jobs. This the spiritual-minded man was willing to do. But he felt he could do nothing lasting until the present owner realized what had happened and was willing to work along with him. After some meetings and long talks, during which the business daily grew worse, the new owner became convinced that there was something to the former owner's theory.

So the former owner set to work. He left his ranch home and took a room at a downtown hotel for the sole purpose of intensive prayer and spiritual work, in order to prepare himself to properly *speak the word.* At home, he explained, there was so much to be done and so many pleasures that his mind was too divided. He had to do intensive work. So to town he went, to a room alone. Every morning he called in the salesmen and the owner to brief them on spiritual laws, what had happened, and what needed to be done. From the first the owner and his salesmen all felt better, but none of them minimized the approaching crisis. They had to raise several hundred thousand dollars or close the business. In his hotel room, Mr. Potter (not his name) concentrated on the problem with all he knew of spiritual laws. A whole week went by and not a dollar seemed to have come to the company.

"It will come and in time," the older man said, calmly.

On the ninth day Mr. Potter went down to the hotel dining room for dinner. He felt led to talk to a man he found sitting alone. They were strangers but discovered, happily, that they had mutual friends in New York and Los Angeles. They had read many of the same books, had ideas and interests in common. Most exciting to them both, they discovered their common interest in spiritual laws as a means of running the business of the world. Before they parted that night, the man from the East asked Mr. Potter if he knew of any really good place to invest some money. He had a son-in-law who wanted to come West, and he, the father-in-law, was out looking around for him. In a few days the deal was concluded. The man brought not only his son-in-law and money into the company, but his own wealth of spiritual knowledge and past experience of working with spiritual laws. The owner who had let the business go down was willing to sell out his interest. The salesmen kept their jobs, the business was once again in good hands, and all concerned were happy.

How many idea people do you suppose Mr. Potter sent out? And did they bring back to him according to their kind? They certainly did. Consider these facts about that case:

The new man (let's call him Mr. Eastern) was looking for a place for his son-in-law but had *definitely intended* to go to San Francisco. He "suddenly decided to go to Los Angeles instead." He had *definitely intended to go about it leisurely*, thoroughly, to take months to think it through and plan. But he "got a feeling to get up and go now, at once." He took a plane to Los Angeles. He had been advised by friends to go to a certain hotel and *definitely intended* to do so. But on the plane he talked to a man and then changed his mind. He went to the hotel where Mr. Potter was staying. He had never heard of Mr. Potter before and Mr. Potter had never heard of him.

If we went into all the proof of the power, intelligence, and limitlessness of the spoken word that was revealed about this case as time went on, it would fill a much larger book than this.

Another example:

A man complained that he was good, honest, a lifelong church member, yet he was poor, always had been. He wanted to know why God had let him down.

We discovered he always sent out poor servants to do his work. "An unprofitable servant," I told him, "will keep you broke trying to support him. If you want wealth, you must *send out profitable servants.*"

The man was secretly envious of those who had money. But aloud he talked against the "sinfulness of possessing worldly goods." He was secretly sure that wealth always meant dishonesty on the part of the owner and did not dream this conviction showed through to all he met. He felt sorry for himself and was angry with God without even realizing the fact. After a good deal of instruction on the power of his word and picturing his ideas as living little people, I said to him:

"You have been sending out ragged, unkempt servants. You sent sickly servants as salesmen to ask others to buy your wares. You sent words that asked pity of men instead of admiration of men. Why buy pity when there are pearls to be had? Words are your cash-in-hand capital."

The man, his imagination stirred by the little word people, said, "Oh my God, what shall I do? I have been pouring out a crummy lot, I must confess," and he groaned in self-disgust.

"Change your heart," I advised. "Then try again. Remember, you are a king, a sovereign in your own right. You rule more cells in your body, every one of which is alive and intelligent and amenable to suggestion, than there are people on earth. You have millions of ideas, thoughts, words to serve you. Send them out. But remember, they will always tell the truth about you. If you are afraid, incompetent, unjust, if you lie, cheat, steal, if you are lazy, if you want something for nothing, if you are greedy or selfish, your word people will tell everyone you and they meet all about it. *You cannot bribe, beg, or force your word servants to do anything more than they are.* But you *can* choose which servants you will send out into the world and you will never live long enough to use all that are at your disposal, awaiting your *spoken word* to send them out to work for you."

With first a change of heart (increased consciousness) and a working knowledge of spiritual laws, careful choice in speaking the word for what he did desire, the man altered both his life and his fortunes.

Now to you and your program of speaking the word for increased wealth: Take the three steps already given. Then keep your self in confidence by a process we can call backing up your men in the field. You are the head office. Here are rules that will help you. They are to be studied time and again. This chapter is necessarily the longest in the whole book because it sets the pattern to be used in solving any problem.

1. *Start with the truth.*

The truth about yourself is that you are a king. A soul Self. You have dominion over all the earth except other human beings. With them you must cooperate for the highest benefit of all concerned. You can take advantage of them if they allow you to do so through their fear, or your temporary superior advantage or cruelty or some other cause. But the minute you do so, you have put a noose around your own spiritual neck. Remember the man who thought other people were just "poor fish—another sucker"? Behave like a king! Speak like a king! Think like a good, wise, progressive king! Picture in your mind the highest type human being you can, and then try to speak, think, desire, and do as he would.

2. *Send your princely servants.*

Send forth rich thoughts and ideas richly dressed with gifts in their hands for other kings and princes. Put *growing gold* in their pockets. Now growing gold is a kind of gold that multiplies itself. Putting it into the pockets of your word servants makes it secret, but the reward comes openly. It gives your servants a prosperous feeling so that they impress all whom they contact with rich ideas, achievement without limit, expansion, and growth. Putting *growing gold* into their pockets enables them to buy things and opportunities for you without limit because they can never spend all they have. More is always growing. They will bring back profits to your door of experience along with wonderful people.

Remember, Mr. Potter sent out rich thoughts and they brought back a rich man.

Here is a princely idea he used repeatedly: *Infinite Mind is my real resource, and I am unlimited because*

God is unlimited. He spoke those words aloud thousands of times. Not to convince God but to convince himself—to continue to walk toward his goal.

3. *Send out your truth-seeing servants.*

"I see God's plenty everywhere
And God will give me my full share."

That servant was sent out by a man who needed money and who got it. It is a twin idea. You cannot long use such words as *plenty*, *my*, *share* without filling your consciousness with the awareness of the abundance of nature and of God. It will increase your faith that will draw plenty to you. Remember that those words are living entities which will go out and lodge in other people's minds, will collect other thoughts on the way, will even stimulate the dormant thoughts already in your mind. They will behave fully in accord with their character and they *will always come home to you*, completing the cycle. So it is up to you to see that you send out only just such profitable servants.

4. *Send your enthusiastic servants.*

Enthusiasm is a combination of desire and faith. It is happiness, born of surety of success of a project, and is a form of advance rejoicing over the good that is to come. It reaches out to the other fellow and wins his support. All people like to be on the winning team. Enthusiasm is an advance sign of success. If you are not enthusiastic about your work, either change jobs or find in the job you have the points about which you can become most enthusiastic.

Example:

A friend of mine does spiritual work for her husband so thoroughly that he is one of the most successful men in his field on the West Coast. She gave me the following as one of the parts of success. She did not know where it originated, and I have not yet learned. But the author deserves honor as one who has presented a truth about life. She said:

"He who whispers down a well
  About the goods he has to sell,
  Will never reap the golden dollars
  Like him who shows them round and hollers."

Don't send your word servants down a well—send them out into the world where they will "holler" and call attention to you and your worth with enthusiasm.

Here is a servant that will prove profitable for you:

"I love my work and my work loves me.
  We are a winning team, you see."

5. *Send out servants who know their facts.*

If you do not know the facts of your business or profession, your words will tell the world that you do not. No amount of bluffing and pretending will take you through. Your seeking, asking words are unlimited. Facts presented break down resistance and, by over-coming fears, carry you toward your goal. Facts laid down become a bridge over the gulf between you and your prospect or buyer, over which he will walk to meet you halfway to hear your story. When you get him that far, you can convince him of your proposition if it is a good one. Be fair. You cannot be unfair to him without being unfair to yourself.

6. *Send out servants who are patient.*

Hurry indicates fear. When we rush people, we are afraid in some degree. And we arouse fear in them to a like degree. The Bible tells us that "he who makes haste with his feet misses his way." We do not like people who rush us, because we do not like to be afraid. The instant fear comes, we start to walk away from God—start to lose faith in life. The high-pressure salesman is always having to move on to new territory. He never builds a clientele. Never be hurried into signing or buying anything. The hurrying salesman is fearful that you will not sign. The better his goods or proposition, the more he wants you to know about it. He has time to tell you and wants you to take time to learn about it.

7. *Send out industrious servants.*

Watch out for the idle-word servants. A man who was failing in his profession began to prosper when he stopped his long, idle conversations with men who just dropped in for "little visits" that wasted hours of time. I pointed out to the man that his friends were bringing him their loafers and featherbed boys, who just went along for the ride. The man then brought out his own idle servants and they all had an unprofitable time. They were unconsciously justifying their failures in their negative talking, blaming others. The man found that by having a definite plan or schedule, he could easily say no to the time-wasting friends. He learned to say:

"I am supporting my profession, and my profession is now supporting me."

8. *Send out peaceful servants.*

If you are quarrelsome in your nature or with your job or with the world, your word people will bring back turmoil to you. Example:

A woman in business had been doing well but started to lose customers, and this at a time when she wanted to sell the business. She came for help, saying: "The trouble is, I am no longer interested in it. I have to fight myself to go down and unlock the door every morning. It is humdrum drudgery. I have come to hate the business, even the people who come. I'm trying to sell it but no buyers have come. I ought to be in creative work."

We discussed the fact that all people are creators. Some create tragedies, ugliness, poverty. Others create beauty, happiness, fortunes. Each of us must choose what we will form, good or evil. Otherwise, without deliberate choice, we land in middle ground and create confusion, frustration, and chaos that can eventually kill us. But long before that extremity, it will make us poor, sick, or mentally ill. The stern law of life says: "Choose this day whom you will serve." I told her: "You have been choosing to create war with yourself and your possession. Now choose peace. Send out peaceful servants, and a buyer will be attracted to your store. Sell it, then get into a business you like better."

She could not at first go along with me, she said. But by continued teaching, she began to see. "By your disturbed thoughts you are warning prospective buyers to stay away. You are saying there is no happiness here for you. No profit here. All the world wants happiness. A buyer must be looking for a profit if he is to buy your shop."

The woman sent out this servant:

"I am at peace with all the world, and all the world is at peace with me."

Added to this she sent out simply thousands of thoughts a day about what someone could do with that business, someone who would love it and put his mind to it. "For the right person it would be a gold mine," she both saw and said hundreds of times a day.

A buyer came. The deal was closed. Then the new owner said: "I felt peaceful and sure the moment I walked in the door. I have big plans for this place. It is a natural for me. Don't ever worry, thinking you sold me a lemon. To me it is a gold mine."

Peaceful servants allow those whom they contact to relax and think, to come to conclusions, to build up new plans and dreams. We believe in our decisions made with a mind at peace with ourself and with the world.

9. *Send out self-possessed and poised servants.*

Fear of not enough is perhaps one of the greatest problems of modern man. For the past thirty years the world has been so filled with thoughts of "financial insecurity" and we have heard these words so often that their idea has gone more deeply into our race consciousness than many of us might realize. Such ideas will prove to be troublemakers in your household. Get rid of them. Never send them out to represent you. They are jittery, unhappy, fearful, distrustful, noisy servants. Send out peaceful, sure servants. Such as:

"My God will feed my every need according to His riches."

A woman who had been ill and on charity was trying to make a double comeback. She used this affirmation as her "chief servant." She would walk to the rhythm of it. She went to bed thinking it, expecting God to take care of her. Her health was completely restored and she got a job. "I will use that truth the rest of my life," she told me gratefully.

If you need more money, a better job, appreciation where you are, a promotion, or new ideas, try the above servant. Send it out. Sing it out into the world. Walk, march to a tune of it. Let your tires sing it as you drive. If you feel you do not have faith in God at this time, then accept my faith. I offer it to you here and now. I work every day in prayer, love, and faith, and speak the word for all people who are reading my books and are honestly trying to get help from them. Accept my faith. Just say, "Your God will feed my every need according to His riches," and say it whether you believe it or not, at first. Persist and the belief will come. Remember, I will be sending my word servants to help you.

A man who was using the above Truth statement to build his consciousness for increased income delighted in adding words to it, embodying various things he wanted and many he did not really need. His added lines included, "Coat and vest and all the rest, including stout new britches." Every morning he walked to the tune of it on his way to the bus. One morning he overslept, "the only time in my whole life, I think," he told me. He had to take a later bus. A woman was sitting there who "seemed so sad and discouraged looking that I hoped I could cheer her up and sat down and started talking to her," he reported.

Before they arrived downtown the woman had told him that her husband had died some six months before and that she had not been able to give away his clothing, but now she wanted to give it to someone who wore the same size in every item that her husband had worn. The man was given a number of fine suits, "coat and vest and all the rest," and there certainly were a number of pairs of "stout new britches."

The man did not actually need clothing but he needed a larger income and so needed increased consciousness. He accepted the widow's gifts with gratitude, recognizing them as "signs of land," he said. Not long after, he made the demonstration he had set out for.

You try it: "My God will feed my every need according to His riches."

10. *Send out healthy servants.*

It is a spiritual sin to send out thoughts of sickness, ill-health, and complaints into the world. It adds to the total of sickness-smog. And like all else that we send out, it comes back to us. We will not go into this point here, since the next chapter is devoted to health.

11. *Send out disciplined, trained, confident, and courteous servants.*

Send out: "I *can*, I *know*, I *should*, I *ought*, and I *will.*" Do not send a boy to do a man's work. Do not send out servants that feel inferior. Send a rich word to do a rich job. Send out *"please"* and *"thank you, sir."* Send out praises and prayers. Send out servants who praise, build, cheer, encourage others. Send out servants who have an *attitude of gratitude* about all life.

Example:

A man who was certain he deserved promotion in his company but was disappointed three years in succession, while other men not so capable went ahead of him, asked me to tell him frankly what was wrong with him. "I can't go on blaming everybody but myself," he said. Consultation revealed the fact that he had a habit of what he called "only light-weight swearing." He would say, "Oh, the hell with that." Or, "What the devil do you mean?" in ordinary conversation. He was also rather proud of some of his most descriptive words which caricatured his boss and fellow employees. He often amused himself by thinking about them. When I pointed out to him that he gave them the feeling he was always laughing at them behind their backs, he said: "I am. But hell, old Mason (not his name) does have ears that stand out like the handle on a teapot." He had a large stock of such thoughts and vivid descriptions of his associates.

He was earnestly seeking to learn, so I gave him a quick lesson he badly needed and which I felt he could bear. After giving him a long, silent look, so filled with destructive criticism that he began to react to its power at once, I said things to him that were in kind. As I spoke he seemed to shrink. His face, his whole body, revealed his hurt. Putting his hands to his face as if to ward off blows he said, "Don't!"

He had come for help. He knew I was only giving him a lesson and yet he was so affected by what I said that it took me more than an hour to build him up after I had torn him down. I suffered almost as much as he did. But he got the lesson.

"You must remember, other people hear your thoughts," I said. "Think people up, not down. Everyone has a great many faults. It is their job to correct them, not ours. Our job is to see the best in them."

The man made a practice of silently saying to the people in his office, "I behold the Christ in you, in all you say and think and do." Their attitude toward him started to change for the better. I wrote in his life notebook:

"Every curse is a step in reverse,
    Every word of praise is a step toward a raise."

When the man's promotion came the next year, his superior said to him: "Personality has always been a big factor with us. And you have become one of the most likable men in our firm."

12. *Send charitable and generous-hearted servants.*
People who wish to destroy other people call them harsh names and ascribe to them soul qualities and habits that they themselves hold. Successful American businessmen have borne more abuse in this way than any other group of people in the world. To their everlasting credit, however, they go right on creating new wealth for millions of others and generously sharing their own all the while. America occupies the highest place in the history of man for charity and generosity. It is an ideal any person setting out to create a new fortune for himself might well follow.

A very successful businessman told me his fortunes changed from the hour he decided to let his employees have a larger share of his earnings. Another told me he always paid his church tithe "from the top of the roll."

The point to remember is, when you do give, *give gladly*. Let your gift carry love with it. Then it has no sting.

Believe and say:

"I always have plenty to use and to give.
I will always have plenty as long as I live."

This idea will prove a profitable servant.

13. *Send weather-wise, courageous servants.*

Many business people have told me that their success was due to the surmounting of some crisis in their affairs. There is always a rainy day in business and in private life. Sometimes it turns out to be a flood. But send out servants who know how to survive and operate successfully in stormy weather. One man learned to say:

"Showers of blessings are falling on me.
I claim as my own all the good that I see."

It enabled him to see good where before he had not. The law says we may claim for our own as much as we can see, believe in our heart, and accept in our consciousness. The man learned to turn seeming defeat into unusual success by sending out the idea that good was coming to him in showers. People began to admire him for his courage, see worth in him they did not see before. New opportunities "showered down on him," as he said. He came to believe what he said.

14. *Send grateful servants.*

A very wealthy woman whom I knew for many years was also one of the most grateful. When I would phone her and ask, "How are you?" she always replied, *"The Lord has been good to me."* Then she would tell me about the happenings in her life and in the lives of the members of her family. She was born poor and so was her husband. She had enough gratitude for both of them. Her spirit went out before them and opened the way for them to earn a fortune. She was an ordinary, everyday type of woman, with no special education or talent. But she had a happy heart, a grateful heart, and she expressed her gratitude every day of her life. *The Lord has been good to me* proved a profitable servant who went out for her and brought back dollars, stocks and bonds, real estate, good rentals, good tenants, good business judgment, good friends, good family relations, a good long life. She left several million dollars when she passed on.

Remember: *Every one of your servants has two parents.*

Every idea to which you give birth by speaking it into the world has two parents: your heart and your present purpose. What is in your heart now? A collection of beliefs about poverty? Ideas of scarcity, limitation? Any hate there? Any thoughts or convictions of inability or weakness? Search well and see whether you have any enemies in your own household. If so, throw them out! Choose and send only the good and profitable servants out into the world of men and ideas around you.

Look again at the Bible quotation at the head of this chapter. Think it through. The windows of heaven are not in the sky. Heaven is harmony. When we are harmonized with God, we are harmonized with all men, including ourself. We can then hear and make ourself heard. We are then consciously unified with all there is. We ask for what we want and receive it. We can never get away from the necessity to keep our heart with all diligence, for truly, out of it come the issues of life for the individual. He is as rich or as poor as his own ideas about himself, other men, God, all life.

Again: God is in heaven. "The kingdom of God is in the midst of you," said Jesus. The *windows of heaven are also in the midst of you.* Your need is to see what is within you, and to work from that within out. Think it through a moment. We are too busy looking for something outside ourself. The Bible is one long repeated phrase about the power of our own thought that is within us and that we set into motion by our spoken word. This does not mean that thought waits for our spoken word in order to work. It works instantly, constantly. That it precedes speaking is the point we wish to make. When God opens up the windows within us, our thoughts and words are powerful indeed. So much so that they go out into the world and bring back so much of worldly goods—gold, silver, things—that there is not room enough to hold them. We have to put others to work. Taxes take a great proportion of it. Anyone using this promise to the full will find himself a center, like the hub of a wheel, which will send out a stream of wealth into the whole world, like spokes on the wheel. The rim of that wheel will become his natural orbit.

The Bible verse is tied in with tithing. (Read the verses preceding it.) The tither is one who has reached a point of no fear concerning the future. Many people tithe and remain poor all their lives. They are giving from a sense of duty or fear, or both. Moreover, they continue to believe in poverty as the normal state of man. But the true tither gives ten percent, knowing he never will lack the ninety percent. He is the one who makes millions.

In doing research on a number of founders of American fortunes, I was struck by the fact that they all had two things in common: *fearlessness* and *a dream.* Not one of them had set out to make money, but rather to do something that meant a lot to them. Money followed naturally. They were not averse to creating a fortune, but it was not their main objective. James J. Hill wanted a railroad stretched across the United States. Henry Ford wanted to make an automobile so inexpensive that the average family in America could own one. Great inventors were trying to get something done that interested them.

If you have a dream that you want to see realized, *speak the word for it*. If not, then find a job big enough for you to do, one that badly needs doing. When you get the big idea, thank God for it and go to work, remembering God will win more than you when you make your dreams come true.

Use Wonderful Words of Life

Only say the word, and my servant will be healed (Matthew 8:8).

Out of the abundance of the heart his mouth speaks (Luke 6:45).

He cast out the spirits with a word (Matthew 8:16).

The more I work with spiritual laws, the more I am convinced that the sick body nearly always indicates a sick self.

To heal the body without healing the self as, for example, with a physical operation, is often to find sickness reappearing in some other part of the body or the mind—or the return of the former complaint. In a more enlightened tomorrow the doctor will start with the self of his patient, asking, "Why do we find sickness here at all?" instead of starting with the body and asking the patient: "How do you feel? What are your symptoms?"

There is one symptom which always indicates self-sickness. And that one unfailing symptom is *unhappiness*.

Unhappiness, I am convinced, always leads to sickness of the body or mind if persisted in long enough. It always leads to disturbance and destruction of some kind. Unhappiness is a warning that should be heeded. It is a step toward death.

In an issue of The First Methodist Messenger, this

news item was reported:

The American Public Health Association, meeting in Buffalo, heard the report of a study made by two professors in Cornell University's medical college which indicates that unhappy, ineffective, and upset persons make up about one third of the population of the United States. This third, it was said, fills the divorce courts, crowds the hospitals, overloads the welfare agencies, and burdens industry with a staggering cost of accidents and absenteeism. The professors based their conclusions on a study of the health records of 2,824 workers. Unhappiness, they said, is so costly that further research on the matter would be profitable to society.

The staggering cost to the other two thirds of the population, who have to live with and pick up the pieces of the unhappy destructive third, can never be counted. The reader need not wait for society to carry on further research as to what unhappiness is and does, and how to avoid it. The Bible tells him.

Unhappiness is the result of a heart that is filled with a mixture of ingratitude and fear, which gives rise to all manner of frustrations, anxieties, animosities, and desires to strike back. It dictates words and deeds that bring reactions from others that intensify the unhappiness. "Hope deferred makes the heart sick," says the Bible. When the heart is sick we are sick all over.

"Hope deferred makes the heart sick" because we were born for bigger, more splendid and satisfying experiences in life than most of us ever meet. We never get over hoping for the wonderful things of life that we always know, in our secret heart, are ours by divine right. Then, if in childhood we start to fill our heart with notions, beliefs of fear, anger, feelings of inferiority, and with all the negative thoughts that manifest in our life later, we find ourself in deep conflict of desire between our potentials and our everyday life.

A king is supposed to have a right to the best of everything the world affords. Each of us is a king, a sovereign, in his own right. But we don't always remember who we are, what we are, why we are on earth, who sent us, and where we go when we leave here. When we forget these truths we live under a cloud. We set up a vicious circle and whirl around in it until we are sick—sick of ourself, of living, and of the world.

The symptoms of the sick heart are negative thoughts, words, desires, convictions of the sufferer. I term them the "neggies." They are killers. If we are to get well and stay well, we must certainly *choose* and *use* wonderful words of life—words that are filled with the wonder and joy of living. Words that lift the spirit. Words that remind us of our potentials. Words that have a song from the heart, that sing of the greatness of the individual and of his power and might because he is a child of God! Words that constantly remind us of our destiny, that our real home is heaven. To choose and use wonderful words of life will set up a benevolent and ever-enlarging circle in which we can travel on and on to greater and greater livingness. For as we speak our word out into the God-Mind around us, the thing, the experience, the condition which it declares will make its circle and come back to us.

Example:

A man who was ill came to me for help. Among other troubles the doctor had told him he had sugar in the urine and that he would have to stop "flying off the handle," become calm, control his emotions, and be more joyful, or he might expect serious ill-health.

"What is it," I asked him, "that you are so unhappy about? What is it you have always hoped for that has been denied you, or that you have not yet achieved, that keeps you silently angry most of the time?"

He sat looking down at his clenched hands, struggling to control his emotions.

"What is making you so heartsick?" I persisted.

Tears ran down his face, choked his voice, as he said: "Everything. I'm sick of life."

As we got under way with questioning, the facts were revealed: he was worried, hurried, in debt, unhappy at home and at work, sick of trying and failing. Things on earth were not what he had hoped they would be.

"You are disappointed in life," I said. "You feel cheated and resent it. You are angry with yourself for not getting all out of life that you instinctively know belongs to you. Anger is always a defense against fear. You are fearing two things: first, that all your time on earth will go by and there will never be any real fun, happiness, peace, or pleasure in being here. Second, you are fearing what God is going to say to you because you have failed. The fears are subconscious but real. These two make your heart sick. So you are sick all over."

After much more of my explaining, the man understood and agreed. We wrote down a long list of the negative thoughts which he had all his life been sending out into the world, and checked them with the results they had brought back to him. I said: "You have created one negative circle after another until now you are living in a vicious circle of your own making. But you can break that circle by starting a benevolent one."

The man was too tired and sick to concentrate on what I wanted to say to him, so I showed him what to do instead. I took him into the bathroom and after I had filled the washbowl, which is perfectly round, almost full of warm water, I lathered soap into it until it was filled with soap bubbles. Placing my hand in the bowl at the back, I said, "This is what you *are* doing," as I whirled my hand rapidly to the left.

"The soap bubbles represent the affairs of your life," I told him. "Notice that the bubbles are on the surface.

My hand, which is *creating the current*, is beneath the surface. It represents cause. The bubbles follow the current; they cannot do otherwise. They are carried along by the movement of the water. This *is a vicious circle.*"

As he watched, puzzled but willing to learn, I changed the motion of my hand, whirling it to the right, or clockwise in direction. "This is the way you *should* do it, always to the right. But notice that at first the bubbles go neither right nor left. They are in a state of confusion. This is what happens when we use idle words, first for our desires and then against them. But now see, the bubbles are starting to follow the current. We have now set up a circle. This is a *benevolent* circle. Now, you try it," I said, and stepped back.

The man rolled up his coat sleeve, turned back his shirt cuff, and went through the experiment as I had done while I instructed him. As he shifted from the left to the right motion, he said, "If my wife ever caught me at this, she'd say, 'How silly can a man get?'"

"Silly enough to be sick," I told him. "Silly enough to be dizzy, punch-drunk with the problems of his own making."

We went back to my study and I told him briefly:

"You can build up your heart over a period of time, so that it will be so full of faith and love that you can speak your word with such great authority that the very walls of your room will tremble. But first, you must resurrect your consciousness. We can so kill our consciousness to the great miracle of what life is and how to work with it that we have to raise it from the dead. We can so fill our heart with troubles, problems, negative thinking that we are dead on our feet, simply going through motions previously set up."

"That's me," he sighed. "Well, how do I start to change all this?" he asked hopefully.

The man's instructions included the ideas that have

been covered in all my books, plus the ones here. He used the formula for speaking the word that we gave in our previous chapter. The work reported here had to do with his fourth step, or walking toward his goal.

In his case, he was always to move toward the right by *speaking words of life.* The right side is harmony, is creative and progressive good. Speaking to the left is taking steps toward death. I told him: "Every time you say, 'I am worried, I am sick, life is unfair, people do not understand me, I'm helpless in the situation,' you are using words that embody ideas of death. You must awaken your whole self, your consciousness to the wonder, the miracle of life."

We wanted to fasten the idea of benevolent circles in his mind, and so began with the circle of his watch as he wound it every morning. At each turn of the stem he was to say: "Life, life, life." He was to remember: *Every word I speak today will make a circle and come back to me.*

The student is always required to obtain a large hard-cover loose-leaf notebook and a supply of plain white paper. He makes up the story of his new life as he goes along. Into his book go his affirmations and various instructions and notes. Some of the reminders I typed out for him were:

"I will speak words of love and laughter,
And only good can follow after."

"Put a song from your heart in every word you speak," I wrote for his book. "Your words will find it no load to carry. They will come back to you and make your heart sing with gladness. *Carry a tune in your heart and your worries will depart.* Let your blood sing. Let your mind sing. *You* sing. *Sing a song of gladness and drive away all sadness.*"

There were many others. A few more were: "Every

83

little cell is now happy and well." "Sing for life and life will sing for you." I told him, "Join the human chorus. Be a part of the song that God is singing."

The one he liked best and started to use first was:

"My God will heal my every pain
And take me back to health again.
This is a truth that I well know,
And I am grateful it is so."

On the page with it I wrote, "Here is what it does for you: It establishes you with God as the source of all life. Removes fear and blame. You have walked in the direction of death, but now God is going to take you back to health again. This is a truth about God and about you and about the laws of the universe and how they work. You cannot stay healed unless you are grateful, for the ungrateful heart will send out sickly thoughts that will come back and lodge in the heart and sicken the whole body. Saying you are grateful time after time will help to make it so. It is a constant reminder that you should be grateful."

The man used many kinds of circles to match up with his affirmations and jingles of truth. The wheel of his automobile made rapid revolutions that sang to him, "God . . . God . . . God . . . " as the tires hit the seams in the pavement. And: "All is God. All is good. All is well. I am well."

For the morning or night meditation (a twenty-four circle) he used such statements of truth as: "God created this world. He created me. He must have a purpose for me. He must be more anxious for me to succeed than I can be because He knows more about the plan. God has a place and a work for me or I could not exist—I could not be."

The man had been bitterly critical. He was required to copy: "A gentle tongue is a tree of life, but perversement in it breaks the spirit" (Proverbs 15:4). And to say, "Lord make of me a wholesome tree."

People began to change their attitude toward him. This so stimulated him that he earnestly concentrated on trying to create benevolent circles. At night he would ask himself, "What did I set loose into the world today?" thinking, "It will come back to me."

He used this one at least once a day:

"I am straightening out my life
With my wonder words of life.
I will speak to friend and wife,
With my wonder words of life."

He learned to praise God, to compliment people, to praise his wife for her cooking, her beauty, her work, and her wisdom. He learned to lift his eyes to the skies and thank God for life, wonder-filled life. This was the time when the styles for women's clothing changed radically; short skirts gave way to quite long ones and the stylists referred to them as "the new look." The man said he was wearing the "new listen," for he was listening now to every word he said. He was asking, "Is this in tune with the music of life, with the song of life God is singing of man?"

Great improvement was shown from the day he said: "I no longer feel helpless, hemmed in. When things go wrong now, I know why they do. When the good comes, I know I have asked for it, have set it into motion myself. It is almost like being God."

That is exactly what the Bible teaches—that man has the power to decree a thing and that God honors his request.

It is not enough to change the conditions in one's life. A program must be taken up which will keep the changes and grow on to more and even better ones. The time came when I advised the man to join the church he had been attending, and to sing in the choir. To help him in his thinking about singing, I related the following incident to him, concerning my own life:

"When we were children, an epidemic of typhoid fever broke out in our town and many people died of it. My younger sister and I were stricken, and for weeks our lives were despaired of. Many times I would be roused up from an almost unconscious state by hearing my mother quietly singing a church hymn. One of her favorites was Wonderful Words of Life. Mother must have sung it every day during those weeks when we were hardly conscious of self or surroundings. When I heard her singing, I always thought, 'Mother is not worried about us. We are getting well.'

"Later, when we were well, I asked her why she sang to us. She said that, in praying about us, she received the directive to sing to us gently and that the first time she tried it, she noticed such a change for the better that she kept up the practice as long as we were ill."

The man accepted my thought that humanity is a song God is singing and that each individual is a word in that song. He joined the choir and found great relief and hope in singing. It made him happy "just to feel that I belong to something worthwhile."

The fact that the outer man had been ill, that it took him some time to get the flesh cloak he wore completely well, did not gainsay the truth—that he was a Word of God, pure Spirit, which could and did change the outer man. When he sent out those thoughts, he was separating the fact from the truth. Facts are but temporary. Truths are eternal. The truth freed him from the fact (illness) that had bound him.

I have long advised sick people to sing and if too sick, then to listen to inspiring music and let their whole being—body, mind and spirit—take up the harmonies. Sick people are unhappy people. Singing restores happiness. William James, sometimes called the father of psychology, is authority for the statement that we do not sing because we are happy, but that we are happy because we sing. Singing helps us to remember God, to remember that we are perfectly safe and that we are not alone. It does this for the same reason that a wise and loving mother singing to her baby is able to comfort it into peace by giving it a sense of security in love. There is no other security in all the world except love. Man is secure because of God's love. Singing reminds him of that fact.

Let the reader make the test for himself. Start to sing and watch your happiness level rise. When you stop singing in your heart, you pull the connection of awareness of God which is within you. We all ought to sing in gratitude for life. I think we should sing without ceasing in the same spirit that Paul tells us to pray without ceasing. It releases tensions and leaves our mind open and receptive to great and good ideas that are in the air all around us, ready to come into our heart and mind to build, heal, and bless us.

Another example:

A woman who had been in the medical world all her life had an illness and learned she must forever after be calm, peaceful, and good-natured, or be in danger of the return of the destroying illness. She had read my book on love and said: "You are more right than perhaps you know; we must absolutely love or perish, and soon every doctor in the country will be telling his patients (with a certain disease) exactly that—love or perish."

In telling me about her life and work, and in comparing her medical facts with my spiritual ones, she said wistfully: "But what can we do? Life is filled with situations that arouse fear in us. The body knows nothing about the cause of fear. It just reacts to it. When fear comes, the inner works of the body get the message: Hey, there's a saber-toothed tiger out here!

Get ready to fight or to flee! And the machinery inside starts to turn and churn, even though the tiger is only a bill collector or some blonde making eyes at your husband. What can we do in our modern world with some kind of tiger at every bend of the road?"

"Yes, there was a time," I said, "before the advent of Christianity, when the sight of a tiger did mean fight or flee. Psychology, generally, still teaches that. But Jesus the Christ Man gave us a new way to handle tigers. We are to stand and agree."

"While the tiger eats you up, blood raw?" she asked smiling ruefully.

"Overcome fear and you will not flee; overcome fright and you need not fight," I said. "Don't fight or flee. Bring the tiger in and you both have tea."

She asked me to write out something for her to remember, and I did. Later, I handed out the following version to another who had tiger trouble.

" 'There's a saber-toothed tiger out here,
Get ready to fight or to flee,'
Said the cave man of old,
But I am more bold.
I bring him in, and we both have tea."

It is not so nonsensical as it sounds. It is saying that there is a power within man that can overcome any problem he meets in the world outside himself. What man needs to do is to learn how to use the power, time after time and day after day. If he uses it until it becomes second nature to him, he will not flee from the tigers that beset his path. He will make friends with the new situation that looks like a tiger. Finally, when he uses the power of his word long enough, he will find that there are no more tigers. For when there are no tigers in the heart, there will be none on the path. When man learns to use the power God gave him, he will stop having caveman reactions to modern-day situations. He will be saying with Paul, "I can do all things through him [Christ] who strengthens me."

"But you haven't touched on my problem," someone may be thinking at this point. Here are some general hints on health that will help you, no matter what the health problem may be.

1. If you are ever told that you have an "incurable disease," ask yourself: "Is there anything in this disease that God does not know about? Is there anything bigger than God?" Of course not. Then if you feel you do not have faith enough of your own to work on the problem, get someone to work with you. Remember: "With God all things are possible."

2. When we heal the self, the body will heal itself or tell us what to do about it.

3. Never underestimate the power of prayer. In California, William R. Parker, director of the speech clinic of the University of Redlands, set up a prayer therapy project to see what could be done about healing by means of prayer. People who attend it promise one thing—to pray. They must spend a definite amount of time in prayer each day even when the time must be broken up into five- or ten-minute periods, owing to other duties of the patient. I have talked with some of the people who have been healed there. People are healed by prayer everywhere. As before mentioned, there is a movement alive in all Christian Protestant churches today to bring healing back into the church where it once was, and rightfully so. This is not to say anything against medicine or against the medical profession. It is rather to point out the fact that hundreds of thousands of physical and mental healings have taken place in churches through prayer.

4. Make up strong affirmations of Truth that will, when spoken and thought about, sink into your subconscious and there start to change your health and

life. The Bible is filled with these statements of Truth. Proverbs and the Psalms are rich in them. Example: "God is the strength of my heart," sang the Psalmist. Any person who is ill can well sing with him.

5. The following affirmations have helped many known to me. Try them out for yourself:

"God is in charge of my life. All is well with me, and I am well with all."

"Let the same Spirit be in me that was in Jesus Christ."

"Every cell in my body is singing; with health and joy their voices are ringing."

Remember, the creative idea is: *Say it is so!*

Leave Word with the Man
at the Door

Do not be deceived; God is not mocked, for whatever a man sows, that he will also reap (Galatians 6:7).

Do not be overcome by evil, but overcome evil with good (Romans 12:21).

Few of us will attempt to break even a dangerous bad habit until we have suffered enough.

Example:

A man came to me and said he couldn't live with his fears any longer and was going to have to do something about them or, he said, "I will wake up some morning and find myself dead," meaning suicide.

The man had been in prison, but was now out, and things were going badly. He was edging back toward habits which had sent him to prison in the first place. We can call him Steve, which was not his name. But before we go into his story we must, in order to learn the most possible from it, take a well-rounded view of the whole subject of habits.

The difference between success and failure in life is largely a matter of the difference between the established habits of the one who fails and those of the one who succeeds.

Both success and failure are the *harvest of habits.* Words and thoughts are the seeds sown. Deeds that spring from the seeds are the plants that grow and grow. There is always a day of reckoning, a harvesttime. The fruit of the habit then stands forth as good or evil.

Habits of ever-expanding life produce success, happiness, and the good life on earth. Habits of evil hold us back on our march toward God and tend toward death and destruction. "The wages of sin is death." There is no way to avoid the payoff. We cannot get around the law of cause and effect. There is no way to take the power out of our own word.

We often think of the extreme harvest of bad habits as prison. But it is suicide more frequently than anyone who has not done research on the subject could well imagine. Between the beginning of a bad habit and one of the extreme terminals, there often stretches a very long misery road.

Let's listen to an authority on this subject:

"In my fifty years as a law enforcement officer it has been my observation that almost without exception every offender started his career of crime because of a bad habit which began somewhere in that person's life, generally in his early childhood. It has also been my observation that those who have corrected their erring ways have done so by replacing their bad habit with a good one."

Those are the words of Eugene W. Biscailuz, a sheriff of Los Angeles County, California, for many years. The Los Angeles County sheriff's office is the largest in the world in area of square miles, population policed, scope of activities, size of jail, and number of personnel. Biscailuz became internationally famous for his constructive projects with boys' groups, work camps, and for his general rehabilitation programs that trained rather than punished, and paid off for all concerned, including the taxpayer. The sheriff's word carried weight. His observations give us both hope and warning about bad habits.

What is a habit? Webster says it is "an aptitude or inclination for some action, acquired by frequent repetition and showing itself in increased facility or performance or decreased power of resistance."

There we have it. The whole difference between a good and a bad habit lies just here: a bad habit shows itself in *decreased power of resistance.* A good habit shows itself in *increased facility of performance.*

Now we can state the law:

Good is accumulative. Evil destroys itself and the host on which it feeds. No one becomes proficient in a bad habit so that he expands and grows and becomes more and more as a human being. Never. This is true on all planes of existence, physical, mental, and spiritual. Cancer, unchecked, destroys itself finally by destroying the body upon which it feeds. Evil thought can and does destroy the mind. Evil intents and purposes out of the evil heart, when unchecked, destroy the whole moral structure. Good is accumulative and so practice makes perfect.

We can take hope. It is easier to create a good habit than it is to create a bad one. Because in creating a good habit all nature works with us. In creating a bad habit we are working uphill, alone, against nature; while we have free will and the rope of cause and effect is often very long, still it has an end.

Both science and religion agree with the observations of Sheriff Biscailuz—the way to break a bad habit is to replace it with a good one. To do this, we need a change of heart. My work has led me to believe that all *bad habits start with unhappiness and with some degree of feeling inadequate to life.* To be unhappy as used here may be considered to contain other phases of unrest and dissatisfaction; and as Webster defines it: "Not cheerful or glad; sad; sorrowful." But also, and most important to note, "mischievous; wanton."

The negative person is an unhappy person most of the time. *He is unhappy because he is negative.* He is a "no" person. What is he saying "no" to all the time? To God. To love. To doing his part in the world. He is refusing, like a balking mule, to come under the law of love. He is a resister. He refuses to cooperate with life. He drags his feet. He will not walk along happily with humanity, will not sing, dance, work, play, and dream of a better world with his fellowmen. He is so absorbed in himself that he never truly gets outside himself. He is complaining so loudly that he does not hear the voice of God or man offering help.

Danger signals that are flashed from the heart of the unhappy, negative, inadequate person are:

1. His almost continuous condemnation of people, conditions, and things.

2. His blaming other people, conditions, things for his unhappiness, his failure, or his lack of some good he desires.

3. His desires, and often outright demands, for something for nothing, all the way from things and services to unearned love itself.

4. His lack of faith in life and himself that registers as weakness and fear to attempt.

5. His lack of gratitude.

Steve, the parolee, was that kind of person. Not yet thirty, he had no lifework, had done a little of many things. As a child he was a grave problem, refusing to go to Sunday school, disliking school, teachers, authority. Because he was an only child, his parents indulged his whims, ran to his rescue every time he got into a scrape. His father, a professional man, "wanted no scandal." His mother, a social climber, "had no time for him." The mother died. Steve fell in love with a fine girl and she married him, but soon discovered his faults. He loved her and wanted to make good. But his old habits of reacting to situations had "decreased his power of resistance." When he needed money, he took it from his employers, sure his father would come to the rescue until he could make good.

But his father was then ill, had little money, and

Steve had to meet his problem himself. He went to prison. His wife stood by him, worked to support herself. But when he came out of prison, she insisted upon their coming west and starting over. Steve would now have to make good or lose her, and he knew it. He did not come to me of his free will. She forced him to come. But from the first he was eager to cooperate and make good. The trouble was, he did not know how. His father, too, had died and but for his faithful wife, Steve was "right up against it."

It took a great deal of preliminary work with Steve which need not be gone into here. We can pick up from the place where he could name his desire: *"I want to be an honest, useful, constructive, and happy person."*

For the second step, that of drawing and holding a picture of his desire fulfilled, Steve had to work with things. He obtained the notebook and paper as required. On the first page he wrote down his named desire as given. In many pages that followed he pasted dozens of pictures of men who had the qualities, the appearances, and some of the possessions he desired. Cut from magazines, all were in color. Each one showed a man of good character in action. One man stood beside a fine automobile. Another showed a man in working clothes who looked happy and well. Another was being adored by his wife. Another was mowing his lawn, and still another was helping his wife with the dishes. Every picture had a deep meaning for Steve. At the end of the series of pictures he was required to write:

"This is the picture of my vision bright.
Help me, O Lord, to keep it in sight."

When it came to *speaking the word*, or the third step, Steve bogged down. It would have been frustration for him at the time to try to understand the principles involved. Since he had, all his life, looked to others, to things and forces outside himself, both to blame and for help, we had to use some method of looking outside himself. To try to get him to see the Power of his own word, or that he had set up his own vicious circles, or to try to personify his ideas and words as people, would all have been lost on him at that time. But there was a method he could understand and use. I recommend it to all who are chained to a habit they want to break and feel they cannot. It is this: *Cast the burden.* Don't ask more of yourself than you can do. Just cast the burden. Ask for outside help. Ask without understanding anything about what is happening. Just ask with the sure belief that something will help you, take you through.

Let us digress for a moment to learn just what Steve did, why it works, why anyone can call and receive help.

Examples:

A young woman who had become an alcoholic started her healing by asking a large tree in her front yard to take care of her "just for today until I get home again tonight," and by *believing it would do so.* The tree represented strength, moral cleanliness, intelligence, and self-discipline to her. The tree knew how to take care of itself, so it could take care of her, too, she reasoned. The success of any deliberate use of the power of the word or prayer for a definite and specific purpose depends upon faith. The young woman could not at that time believe in God, but she *did believe she would receive help.* She received help which enabled her to hang on and get other help, and she eventually went on to a complete healing. The tree stayed rooted to its spot, of course, but her cry was heard by the Comforter, the Holy Ghost, the Spirit of truth that Jesus said would come into the world upon His leaving.

A young child of five years of age was worried about his quarreling parents. He was especially sorry for his mother. He began to tell her to take his teddy bear to bed with her at night instead of keeping it in bed with himself as had been his habit. When he said, "Tessibee (his baby name for teddy bear) will take care of you and not let you get hurt," the mother was struck by the child's utter faith that his tattered cotton toy could provide safety for her. She was amazed that his idea gave him such comfort that he could go to sleep without it. When she asked him how it was that the teddy bear could protect her, he said in calm confidence, "Because he knows what to do with something." She realized that the child was talking about a truth about life, something he knew by instinct, deeper than reason, and could neither explain nor fully understand. "He was talking about something that exists that we all know vaguely," she reported, "for it took me back to my own childhood when I too knew there was Something, which I had since lost contact with but knew I must now find again or die."

We are all born knowing that there is Something, that very Comforter which Jesus talked about and which is always near us. Even Steve knew it, and there is the place we had to start to work.

To him I said, "You don't know enough yet to handle your problem, and you need a friend who will be with you night and day. So I am going to turn you over to that friend for a while. Later, we will do more work together."

I gave him a picture of Jesus, one of those inexpensive colored lithographs, a reproduction of the painting of Jesus standing at the door and knocking. I told Steve something like this:

"This is a picture of the greatest Man who ever lived on earth. This picture means that He is knocking at the door of the consciousness of every man. He said that if any man would let Him in, He would answer the questions of life for that man, would feed his mind and spirit, would tell him the truth about life that would ever after make him free."

Steve wanted to know whether it was real, and could anyone prove it? I told him thousands had proved it, that he could prove it for himself. We talked about the necessity to believe. Steve was to put the picture up in his room where he would see it the first thing on awakening in the morning, the last thing on retiring at night. Every time he went through his life-story notebook with the affirmations etcetera, he was always to say of his desire, "I ask it in the name and through the power of the Lord Jesus Christ."

"I am not just speaking to a picture?" Steve asked.

"No," I assured him, and told him a number of instances of healing resulting from so casting the burden, from putting the whole problem up to Jesus Christ. "This Man is still alive. He can hear when you call His name. His promise to you will be kept. He will help you. Always ask in His name."

During the day, when a problem arose, Steve was mentally to recall the picture of Jesus at the door and say, "I will turn it over to the Man at the door." When he went to sleep at night, he knew that "the man at the door" would take care of him all the next day. Getting and holding a job presented many problems to Steve, as anyone who ever has been in prison could testify. But Steve had help: "I am not alone. That Man at the door knows all about it."

Of course I worked for him in prayer as did his wife. But Steve worked earnestly, too. At the very outset he had one small experience that was convincing to him about his call for help. It increased his faith. He was totally unhampered, at first, by any thought of being unworthy. *He simply asked for help as his right, and expected help as his due.* If that sounds cold to the reader, let him remember that God gives to us according to His riches and love and not according to our just deserts. All his life Steve had expected someone else to "clean up the mess," as his wife said. He had no trouble on that score in accepting help.

In taking his steps of walking toward his goal, Steve had the able and loving help of his wife who worked with him constantly. He had lists in his book to tell him what to change from and what to change to, for example: to walk away from hate by walking toward love, from resentment toward tolerance and sympathy. Each portion of his bad habits was to be overcome by replacing them with the direct opposite and good habits.

And always that daily: "Tell me what to do today; I ask it in the name and through the power of the Lord Jesus Christ," when he struck a hard spot. When he got a good job, he declared: "Of course. I left word with the Man at the door. I knew it would all be set."

Some of his other affirmations were:

"The Lord is working for me
    To set my mind and spirit free.
    I cast this burden and I go free.
    Lord Jesus does the work for me."

After a long time Steve reached the point of thinking: "Why? Why is it so? Why is it done for me? Who am I to ask? How have I earned such love and help?"

When he began to ask, I knew he was safe forever, that he would go on, alone. And he did.

What about you, dear reader? Do you have a bad habit, or even an annoying one you'd like to get rid of? Then ask yourself some questions: "What am I running from? What do I fear? What is my lack? What do I hate? What am I running toward and why? What do I really hope to have when I get there?"

Then take a stand. There is something *you* must do about it. When poet Don Blanding titled one of his books "Joy Is an Inside Job," he used a statement of Truth about life. Joy is indeed an inside job. Sooner or later the one who is unhappy comes up hard against this fact, that while others can help him to a degree, he must also help himself. You can cast the burden to get started. But life, because of growth, demands of you that you exercise your right to choose. To become the victim of unwanted habits is to become a slave. So make up your mind to use the power of your word to build new habits. *Choose* the good habit and then follow through.

Here are some rules and facts that will help you:

1. Back of every destructive habit is thought out of control. Manage your thoughts or they will control and manage you. Discipline your desires or they will wreck you. Exercise the power to decide or lose the power to do so.

2. Remember that enthusiasm is the lifeblood and quiet contemplation is the backbone, but *good habits are the hands and feet of any successful venture.* Think it through. Good habits are used as hands to hold on to, reach out with, to work with, and they are used as feet to stand on, to walk forward on, to jump up and over obstacles in the way of life. I often tell young parents that good habits will do more for their children's future than money in the bank.

3. Remember that

"An act oft repeated, whether hated or enjoyed,
Becomes a master to be served or a slave employed."

That is one of the affirmations I wrote for a woman who had to break herself of drinking and of lying.

4. There is no power on earth that can make you continue in your bad habits but yourself. There is a power within you that is bigger than anything outside you.

100

5. Remember the steps: Name your desire, draw and hold the picture of the desire fulfilled, speak the word, and move *toward* your goal.

6. "A man protesting against error is on the way toward uniting himself with all men that believe in truth," said Carlyle. When you start to walk toward your goal, you will find that unseen help comes to your aid. It is the accumulated good will in the world, the silent rejoicing of all men, that one more fellow being is now walking toward the right.

7. Break yourself of any tendency to self-pity. It can become deadly. Before you can gain pity you must be a pitiful object. Why become an object of pity? Never say "I am pitiful." That is speaking a powerful word against yourself. The world hears your word, even if you never speak it aloud but only feel it, and the world acts upon your self-condemnation. Every cell of your body hears and acts upon it also. Get a change of heart. Remember:

"A tranquil mind gives life to the flesh,
     but passion [envy] makes the bones rot."
(Proverbs 14:30.)

Work for the tranquil mind. Self-pity is a form of saying, "They are all having a better time than I am," or "They have more than I," or whatever it may be. This keeps away from you the very things you do desire. Besides, it can wreck your physical and mental health.

8. If you have not thought well of yourself, use this affirmation:

"I love God and God loves me.
     I am as safe as a child can be."

Or say: "I love all people, let all people love me," if loneliness has become a bad habit with you. Say:

"Wonderful, speaking, limitless me,
Thank God for the wonderful things I can be."

This strengthens your whole character and outlook on life.

If you have had the bad habit of lying, copy the affirmation below and put it in a place where you will see it a few times. Then throw it away and replace it with some affirmation of your own about telling the truth. "Lies will never take you through; they never fool anyone but you."

9. Finally, if learning and working with the spiritual laws is all very new to you and you feel somewhat as Steve did, then fall back on that never-failing method he used. Cast the burden. Become as a little child. Cry out as a helpless child, but *with the faith* of a trusting child. You will receive help and protection. Try to do your part. But remember that until you can, you'll never be alone with your problems if you will remember to leave word with the Man at the door. And keep on and on until you reach that place where you know how to open the door and let Him in—into your heart and life forever.

Learn to Speak the Language of Love

But from the beginning of creation, "God made them male and female" (Mark 10:6).

But if you do not forgive, neither will your Father who is in heaven forgive your trespasses (Mark 11:26).

Working with people and their problems for many years has convinced me that the biggest need in the world today is not money, armed might, or laws of the land, but love. More human misery, sin, sickness, death, mistakes, and general failure in life result from violations of the law of love than from any other reason. Indeed, I am ready to say than *from all other reasons put together.*

Violation of the law of love is not only the number one problem of the human race, but more and more people are coming to realize that fact and trying to do something about it. Three examples: divorce, crime, war. Each year billions of tax dollars are spent for defense measures. Those billions of dollars are said to be necessary because it is expected other nations are going to break the law of love.

No one needs to be told that crime and divorce are examples of the violation of the law of love. But we all need to be reminded frequently that there is something which an individual can do about it to benefit not only himself but the whole world.

However, our purpose here is not to tell you how to build a better world for all men, but to show you, the individual, how to use the Power of your Word to build a better world for yourself. This chapter is to help you learn how to use that power to win and hold love in your life.

We start by taking another look at the steps we have been using:

1. *Name your desire.* Is it for love? Friendship? Marriage? To hold the marriage you have? To get along better with the people where you work, or in your neighborhood?

2. *Draw a picture of the desire fulfilled.*

3. *Speak the word.*

4. *Take steps toward your goal.*

If we took the first three steps correctly and then did nothing to cancel our order, but in all ways worked with it in thought, word, deed, and feeling, there would be no chance of failure. It simply would be done according to our decree—if we believed. But there is the element of time. While waiting we become anxious, fearful, and so cancel the order we have carefully prepared and sent in. Or we forget that the Power in our Word works through us in all sorts of ways quite as much as it works outside us. Unless we are on guard, we walk away from our goal instead of moving toward it. This brings us frustration, cancellation, and defeat.

To walk toward our goal of respect, friendship, and love, *we must speak the language of love.*

The language of love is any language you choose as long as you remember *to put wings on your words before you let them go out into the world.* In a former chapter we talked about seeing our ideas as living beings, members of the Logos race. We also talked about the fact that we clothe those idea people with the words we use to project or eject them into the world. It will not be difficult for us now to take the practice a few steps further. But we must be sure the wings are on the word before we release them. So begin now to think in terms of putting wings on your words.

This will help you to get started:

"I will put wings on my words
Like the wings on the birds."

We face three questions which we must answer before we can go on.

Our first question is: Why should we put wings on our words?

Well, what is the purpose of wings? To lift, of course. If we are to walk toward our goal, we must *learn to lift the spirit* of those who hear our words, *including ourself.*

Wings help the possessor to go up higher. We all want to go up higher for more of fun and freedom, for more learning, doing, and being. Flying is fun. Drudging through life is misery. Getting down in a rut of living is a tragedy. Wings lift us into great and adventurous living here on earth. Wings remind us that we are children of God almost on a par with the angels themselves. Wings make us feel secure and important today while reminding us of our destiny tomorrow. With wings we trust all our other powers more fully. Everyone wants wings. Then let us remember this law of life:

We will always love and respect the person who gives us wings. Including ourself? The blessed truth is, yes! If we will make a practice of giving wings to our words, silent thoughts about ourself, we will never hate ourself.

Our second question is: Why? Why is all this so? Can we really count on it?

The answer is yes, we can count on it because all the world is hungry for love. No one really feels adequate. Even the biggest never feel quite sure. All have a secret hollow, a secret unfed hunger. The basis of all desire for love and approval, to be understood, is rooted in the desire for the right status with God.

To be right with God is the greatest need in our life. It may never come to the top of our consciousness, but it is always there, below the surface. If God does not approve of us, what is to become of us? This striving to be worthy of God is the foundation on which civilization rests—the wheels on which all progress will roll forward tomorrow.

Therefore we can help others and ourself by remembering this important fact about the nature of man. By assuring another that he is respected, appreciated, loved, approved by us, we help him feel that perhaps he is also approved of God. We can then, by our words and our attitude toward him, remind him that he is a child of God, secure and on the way to becoming a Christ person. We can convince him that he is a good, desirable person. We can and we should *let our word lift him so high* that soon he will develop spiritual wings for himself and do his own flying. To help him become lovable is to help him more than we can in almost any other way. For there is no security for man on earth outside of love. Let us make the following a part of our consciousness forever:

a. We want to be with people who remind us of our worth.

b. Love the highest and the best in people, and you will draw the highest and best people to you. For there is a law which says that we will always draw to ourself that which we secretly and really love.

c. To help others fly is to give *wings to ourself.*

d. Love is the language that frees both speaker and hearer.

Our third question is: How do we put wings on words?

We are speaking the language of love. Love means caring, with all the fervor of which the heart is capable. If we love, we act for the highest welfare of the object of our affection. If we love, we speak from an honest heart. Love must be real to be effective. By our *intent and purpose*, our *real caring*, and by our attitude we put wings on our words. You can take any ordinary word and give it wings by meaning to do so. This is part of the power of decree. Earlier we said we would put wings on our words like the wings on the birds. Birds have two wings. Put those two wings, *purpose* and *attitude*, on your words.

Example:

Recently I saw this happen. A young man, much enamored of a young woman, said to her, "Oh, *you!*" in what appeared to be a banter of words. They were singing at the piano. He gave her a little shove, a gesture of pushing her away. She had been teasing him and he liked it. But he was pretending he didn't, the better to hide his real emotions there in the presence of their young friends. They went on singing with the others. But her blushes were evidence and confession that she had received his real message in those two words. For what he really said in his purpose and attitude was: "Oh, but *you* are different. *You* are beautiful. *You* are the one I love. How wonderful that *you* should pay any attention to me!"

When you learn the language of love, you find that any word can be lovely. The simplest "no" or "yes" can carry hope, more than that, life itself, to the one who hears it. Such words have been given wings by being translated into the language of love.

So learn to use the power of your attitude, intent, purpose, and feelings to give wings to your words. Wings on your words of praise, appreciation, forgiveness, and happy expectancy will carry your message of love to others. Haven't you heard people pay a compliment in words that somehow sounded like a criticism? The words had no wings.

Make this experiment now:

107

Say, "Oh, *you*," and imagine you are saying it to someone you love very much, like the young man we've just discussed. Imagine what the person you say it to will hear. See that your words convey that meaning.

Now say, "Oh, *you*," and make it a bitter criticism, thinking as you say it all the words you will leave unsaid, which are: "Oh, *you! You* are dull. You are dumb, always making mistakes. Why should I count on *you?* You are a failure, always have been, and always will be. Besides, I just don't like you!"

Notice now the difference in how you feel when you put *weights on your words* and when you give them wings. If you will go through this practice, before a mirror, speaking both silently and aloud, giving the most realistic performance you possibly can, you'll learn a lot about what makes some people lovely and what makes others so unlovable.

Let us remember as we go along that we can't continue to put wings on our words to others without sprouting a few feathers for our own higher soaring. And also, words with weights on them that hold others down hold us down.

Before we start into the examples from life, let's make a quick summation:

Learn to speak with a purpose and to make your purpose clearly understood. Let your purpose be to help the one who hears you. This means you will have to consider your intent and purpose when you take any other human being into your thought. Think of whom you speak and to whom you speak, regardless of when or where. Only such care will control the how of your speaking, your attitude. The same rule applies to thinking and speaking about yourself.

Now we are back to our starting ground—the heart. Whatever comes out of our heart starts a circle, vicious or benevolent, that will go out and build or destroy on its journey in the world, and come back to our heart as convictions to our life as events, conditions, and things. What we want is respect, friendship, and love. So we shall have to think, feel, speak from a heart filled with love. If we get the heart right, we will not have to worry about the attitude and purpose. They will be right.

To be sure our word has wings, we can ask ourself before we speak it: "Will it lift and free? Or will it ground and hold back?"

Everyone wants to be free because the purpose of life is growth. This growth always is toward God. There can be no growth without freedom. When we help others to greater and greater freedom in living, we are helping ourself to greater living. Now we are ready for examples from life, to see how these laws work out:

Once my husband and I went to a dinner dance. I had not felt like going but had promised, and so we went.

"What have you been doing to yourself? You look ten years younger than when I saw you last!" said the man who was dancing with me. And he said it exactly as if he meant every word of it. It had been only a few weeks since he had last seen me.

Now, I was not looking ten years younger and I knew it. I had been going through a most trying time with many problems of others put upon my heart as well as problems of my own, with a grave decision to make. And, hard to bear, news of one who had fallen low, one whom I had been trying to help stand high. I had gone to the party feeling rather fagged out. But when my friend spoke to me, the wings of his spirit lifted my spirits high. I simply had to answer him in kind.

"What have I been doing?" I replied. "Why, I have been thinking about this party, about you, about dancing with you again. I love to dance with you because you always make me think I am dancing my best. That is because you lead so expertly," I said honestly.

"Oh, so you like to dance with me, do you?" said my friend, pleased.

Then we both laughed and settled to the happy business of having a good time. As we danced I did feel younger. Was it bosh, cheap flattery? No. We were speaking the language of love. We each had used our power of the word to release some of the "imprisoned splendor" in the other and so, in ourself.

All of us have this splendor, and anything we can do to give it outlet in ourself or in another is working with God on a very high plane. For most of the time we are like a cold, dead log, lying in the fireplace. The log is of no use until a kindling spark sets fire to it. Then it begins to burn, to release the imprisoned heat and light of the sun, serving all within its radius. So we ought all to shine, sparkle, warm, and serve. None of us can afford to miss an opportunity so to serve ourself and our fellow men. If we made a regular practice of it, there would be a great deal more happiness in the world than there is today, which would be reflected in better physical and mental health all around.

Rule to remember:

The person who makes a practice of giving others a lift is never without respect, friendship, and love at any age in life.

The true incident just related is only one proof of that fact. The man mentioned was then past eighty-four years of age. He has so many friends, men, women, and children, who love him that he never knows a lonely moment. They stimulate his mind and that helps to keep his body young and active. He is a living example of the truth that old age need not be a time of loneliness and unhappiness. We had met this remarkable man some time before at a dancing class where he was brushing up on his tango and rhumba technique. His business years were given to growing coffee in Guatemala, but all his life his pleasure has been that of giving happiness to others. Once when I asked him how he had learned so many of the laws of love he smiled and said, "My dear, I was woman-raised." I think it is no chance that his first name is John. The name John means "brotherly love."

An example from the opposite side:

A schoolteacher, past forty and unmarried, has few friends. She is intelligent, keeps up with the world, dresses well, travels widely during school vacations, is generous with her money. But she is lonely. All her life she has been critical. If a child misbehaves in her room she calls the parents in and tells them that they have spoiled their child "rotten and ought to be ashamed." On her travels, she tells members of the tour what is wrong with them and even the guides in charge are told about their mistakes. She is a capable teacher, knows her subjects, stands high in her profession. When she says, "You are wrong on that point," she supports her position with solid facts which prove she is right. Her manner says, "Your stupidity is unbearable to me."

And people find that schoolteacher unbearable to them.

Criticism is hard to take, even justified, needed, friendly criticism. If we want friendship and love, we must handle words of criticism and correction as carefully as we would handle swords, shears, and sharp knives; for these can become death weapons, too, to the spirit of love. They can clip the wings the hearer already has. It takes a highly developed soul to forgive a justified wing-clipping; it takes a saint to forgive a deliberate and brutal wing-clipping. And few of us are saints.

If you desire love and marriage, to hold the marriage you already have, or to marry again after having been left alone, the following rules, reasons, and affirmations will help you walk to the right, toward your goal. But here, as in working with all other everyday problems, we must remember that these symbols and techniques are only to remind us of the tremendous power

God has given us. They are daily aids to help us form habits of thinking and speaking under love, using the power of our word correctly to promote the growth of our own soul and to help everyone we meet along the way.

Rule 1. *Start with yourself.*

Reason: If you want love then you must be lovable. You must be able to love others and be the kind of person others are able to love.

Effective affirmations will help. Example:

"I love life and life loves me.
I am as lovable as a man (or woman) can be."

Loving yourself is not vanity; it is paying homage to God, your creator. Who are we to criticize God's work? If you are not as lovable as you should be, two things will happen: you will discover what is wrong with you, and you will also learn how to correct it. Remember, your words about yourself will be honored—they will take form, come into your life as facts and experiences. *Saying it is so is a form of saying, "Let there be!"*

Don't take on the whole burden for changing things in your life. Say:

"I need not run the entire show,
And I am grateful that this is so."

Calling it silly is wasting time. It is based on truth, law. Follow through, make the idea in it a part of your consciousness and use it faithfully.

Rule 2. *Learn about the basic differences in the spiritual nature of the two sexes.*

Reason: You want to give wings to your own spirit and to the one who is to love you. The more truth you know, the more free you will become of mistakes, wrong moves, and low motives. Facts help you walk toward your goal.

Both men and women are a trinity of body, mind, and soul. Men, the active principle, represent mind above the other two. Men are active—explorers, creators, doers. Women, the passive principle, represent soul more than the other two. Women have stored energy, emotions, memories. Both represent body, the physical and material aspects of life, which acquires and holds.

Affirmation:

"I love the men (or women) and the men (or women) love me;
We are children of God, we both agree."

Reason: You must avoid all quarrels of superiority of the sexes, all the old race ideas of "man's place" and "woman's place" and of one being inferior to the other. Go to the truth, to God's idea of man and woman equal according to their nature as God made them.

Example: A man whose wife had left him after three years of marriage came to me asking for help in "making my wife come home to me." His ideas about women were Pauline, to say the least. He wanted me to "tell her that the Bible says that the whole world was made for the benefit and pleasure of man!"

"But I must also tell her that man, with all his benefits and pleasures, was made for woman," I reminded him. Esoterically, I was telling him a truth, as well as giving him a jolt he needed. For all is made for the soul, including the soul of man, of course. But to woman, the soul principle, the passive principle, *things come.* Man—the mind, active principle—moves out, goes forth, seeks and acts. In the final analysis man is drawn to woman (mind is drawn to soul), because man does in a sense belong to woman.

The deserted husband had not learned anything

about the spiritual differences in men and women. He wanted a perfect marriage. But perfect marriages are "made in heaven," meaning in perfect harmony. It is one in which the husband and wife are joined together on all three levels of their being—physical, mental, and spiritual. In such marriages, the two do become one, and the marriage cannot be broken except by the two involved. The irate husband himself had broken his marriage. By his selfishness he had broken the law of love. He had not been concerned with trying to promote the highest welfare of his wife and so lost his own highest good.

Rule 3. *Learn the differences in the basic spiritual needs of the two sexes that influence and dictate all the needs of body and mind.*

Reason: You cannot treat men and women alike and hope to be happy or give happiness. The basic needs of men and women stem out of their basic spiritual nature, according to the way God made them. To ignore or tamper with these differences and needs is to take steps toward defeat, not only in love and marriage but in health and general welfare, in the way we run a business or a nation. This is a subject deserving volumes all to itself, and can be only touched upon here. There is a growing literature on this.

Some points:

Man's greatest need is to be assured, *"You can."* From this need has grown all our sayings and practices of "building the male ego."

Woman's greatest need is to be assured, *"You are."* That is why we say women cannot be told too often, "You are lovely, you are loved, you are needed and wanted."

Marriage is a partnership, not an individual ownership. Men and women do not, cannot duplicate each other's wisdom, purpose, function, achievements. *They complement each other.* Neither can be completely whole without the other. They can live, make a success of life, but they do not get the full benefit of being on earth and learning, without the experience of living, working together as one unit. This is why in all the man-woman relationships they should seek to build each other in the area of their greatest need. To do this is to assure their meeting common needs together with greater ease and satisfaction. Most of the needs are held in common, but ways to fill them are worlds apart.

Example:

The Browns (not their name) kept each other nervous and unhappy in public. They received a wound at home, took it silently, waited to strike back in public. They had learned that it would hurt worse and last longer if they struck back in public. Once, in my home as guests, they started a word battle. Calling them to one side I said: "This is a play party, my dears, and not a fight arena. In my home, no one may say such hurtful things to another human being as you two are saying to each other. Put up your swords. Put wings on your words, or go home."

They knew I meant it and prepared to leave. At the door I said, "You two had better start to build each other or you are going to tear apart your marriage and find yourselves divorced."

Both had become so expert in hurting the other that they were losing friends and prestige in their circle and were hurting the husband's business as well. There just is no good place left in the world today for people who tear others down in public.

The wife, finally convinced that praise paid more dividends than blame and criticism, began on a program that would raise her husband's opinion of himself. She stopped destroying him and started to build instead by a "You *can*, you *did*, you *are*, you *have*" campaign in private and in public.

Some of her ideas with wings were:

115

"One thing I like about my husband is that he can control both his temper and his drinking. My husband is intelligent and he values his thinking power too much ever to dull it. My husband has perfect balance and discipline in his work and pleasure. One thing I like about my husband is that he is just as courteous and kind to me in our private life as he is in public." All of that came out of the mouth of the "new" Mrs. Brown.

The first few times she talked that way, her husband only stared at her in astonishment, but he soon stopped his critical remarks about her in public. After a few months of her open and silent change to the language of love in both their private and public lives, he said to her one day: "The man who says he understands women is a fool. I was sure I had married a shrew, but I find I have an angel instead. Thank God!"

The Browns reestablished themselves in their high standing with each other and so with the world. After she took the initiative to save their marriage, her husband went along with her. Wives generally are more interested in saving their marriage than are husbands, owing to the difference in their spiritual needs, and because they have more time to devote to marriage. Love and marriage are never a joke to a woman, never a minor matter. It is the most serious business in the world to them, and other business becomes more serious only when they have failed or think they may fail in their first cause. For which all the world, including women, may well give thanks. I read statistics showing that there are some nine million unmarried women in this country alone. There are not enough men to go around. This does not lessen the truth of our statements. It shows what a tragedy exists and it creates more problems than anyone can suspect without research into the situation.

Another example:

A wife complained to me that her husband would

not go out with her socially. When we got into her history, we found that secretly she was bitterly critical of him, "but just in her own mind."

"You cannot think bitterness and hatred all the day and then expect love to come in at the door at night," I told her.

"Oh, but I don't *say* those things to him," she explained, after listing the many annoyances she endured. "He just irritates me so that I think those things when he is gone all day and I am home with the problems and the children, and . . . "

"Your thoughts reach him," I said. "Science has proved this tenet of religion beyond doubt. Thoughts of one person do reach through and influence another person. Your thoughts reach your husband with a terrific force which creates his feelings and moods and determines his actions after that. You are tied together by promises, love, interests, and the children between you that you both love. Your unspoken words have all the power of your Word, your Self. You spend all day sending him messages with weights on them, with swords and barbs that cut, and then expect him to come flying home to you at night with flowers in his hand, a song in his heart, to say nothing of theater tickets in his pocket."

She finally agreed that she was "guilty as charged."

I told her she must get her thoughts and words in her husband's presence and in his absence to agree. She must get her intent and attitude right—to build him. She was to use all her powers of body, mind, and spirit to lift her husband up, to avoid tearing him down in her own thoughts or words. The glance of her eyes, the smile on her face, the clasp of her hand, the thoughts of her mind, the meditations of her heart about him should agree with her winged words. She must speak the language of love with her whole being. "Say it with gestures," I told her.

117

And what was she to say to him? To give him ideas that said "You *can;* you *are;* you *have*" the qualities and habits she wanted him to have. To *say it is so,* remember, is to set the power into motion to make it so.

"I have a lot of spade work to do," she said.

She began with a will and worked as hard at her job as her husband worked in his profession downtown. One day she phoned me to say excitedly: "Oh, it worked! It worked!"

Of course. Law can always be depended upon to work. She was using law.

If you love someone, don't spare the praise! No word of praise was ever lost. It is food for the soul and becomes part of the one to whom it is given. In our modern world of hurry, competition, screams of beware here, danger there, death over here, all of us need extra soul-feeding these days. And husbands and wives, heads of families, need it more than any other group of people.

Rule 4. *Build an overall attitude of gratitude.*

Reason: Gratitude acts as a magnet that draws respect, friendship, and love. Ingratitude is a sign of not enough love.

Example: A man complained to me that he had lost his wife's love to another man who had come into her life. The facts as he told them showed that he had been ungrateful, exceedingly so. I told him: "You didn't lose your wife's love. You threw it away." Ingratitude says: "Take it away. I don't want it."

Rule 5. *Avoid arousing anger in another.*

Reason: Anger is a form of defense against fear. The angry child or adult is trying to defend himself. People will not like us if they are always having to defend themselves against us. For the same reason, we do not like people who are always touchy, always flying off into a fit of anger. They put us on the defensive. In both instances, freedom is curtailed. If you have such a problem in your life or home, the following affirmation will prove helpful:

"Let all turmoil and anger cease,
And make our home a home of peace."

If you yourself have the problem of anger and getting quickly upset, you can change it to say: "Let my turmoil and anger cease; let all my paths be paths of peace." *Say it is so.*

If your home life has been gloomy and you have felt short of happiness, generally you can improve yourself and help every member of your family by making the following affirmation every morning, as soon as you awake:

"Now let me arise and all day shine,
For the Lord is good to me and mine."

Each one should make up his own affirmations to fit his own needs, keeping the rule in mind to *say it is so* of that which you desire.

We don't outgrow love, but we outgrow some of our ideas about love. For we are growing beings. The well-balanced person does not look to love of human beings to fill all his needs. He does not look to another for happiness. He becomes love and happiness in himself.

Some rise so high toward sureness of self and of working with God that they no longer are touched by either praise or blame of other human beings. These reach a place in understanding where they are satisfied with their own praise, and know whether or not they are doing their best, whether they are right with God. When they come to that place, they no longer are dependent upon the love of others, but they have it—in great abundance. They are always grateful for it, hold it as a treasure, and give back as much or more in turn. But the fear has gone, and it has gone forever.

There is one simple fact that we can all remember, one goal toward which we can all strive and, by so doing, help every human relationship we shall ever have, including our relations with ourself; that is to remember often and often that *God is love.* We have seen that in the Power of our Word we have the power of attorney to act as God would act under the circumstances, within the laws of the case. If we treat others as we think God would treat them, we shall not go far amiss. This, of course, is exactly what Jesus said we should do, His highest commandment, to "love one another; even as I have loved you." When an individual starts walking toward that goal, his problems fall behind him. When enough of us walk toward that goal, we shall have a better world.

A powerful affirmation for training in love is this:

Let the mind and the love be in me that was in Christ Jesus.

Speak with Authority

Whosoever shall say unto this mountain, Be thou removed, and be thou cast into the sea; and shall not doubt in his heart, but shall believe that those things which he saith shall come to pass; he shall have whatsoever he saith. Therefore I say unto you, What things soever ye desire, when ye pray, believe that ye receive them and ye shall have them (Jesus in Mark 11:23,24 A.V.).

This book has been addressed to the individual and his problems, but especially to the individual who long has said, "Yes, I'd like to change my own life and the conditions for my loved ones and the world for the better, but what can *I* do?" This person implies that there is little or nothing that he can do by himself. To all such I say, "Shift the emphasis and ask, 'What can I *do*?' and you will find the answer."

So far we have talked about the power of decree, the laws under which it operates and the handling of everyday problems. But now we have come to the most important chapter of all—you and the desire of your heart. Problems are just those everyday experiences we meet up with on the way to obtaining our real heart's desire.

A heart's desire is big, important, something to which we might well devote our whole lifetime. We start out by taking an overall view of the things that are.

The Bible is filled with references to the fact that God tells us not only to contact Him, to make all our wants known to Him, but actually to command Him!

The Book of Job tells us that Job commanded God and that God was pleased with him for doing so. And Job received even more than he had in the beginning.

The Bible quotation at the head of this chapter has for generations stirred the heart, hope, and imagination of readers. Today it is stirring the minds of some of the world's greatest scientists. Many now living believe that in this atomic and electronic age, science will be able to prove that man does have this power which Jesus used and talked about and showed how it works and why.

Man is three persons in one: physical, mental, and spiritual. He therefore has power over nature all around him on each of these three levels. By using all three, he has come to where he is today. Generally speaking, man has lived through the physical age, is passing through the mental age, and is now entering the spiritual age. Of course, there is no separation in the three. We only speak of them as separate to try to understand them.

We now know that for every unit of physical power as human beings we have countless billions of units of mental and spiritual power derived from our God-given Power of the Word. This is what Jesus taught. It is what the prophets, not only of the Old Testament of the Christian religion but of other races and religions, have seen and said.

From Genesis to Revelation the Bible tells us about the *existence*, *nature*, *scope*, and *purpose* of the Power of the Word. Jesus, the great Teacher, used it and therefore spoke as one "having authority." Jesus said that we have this power, too, which is above the physical earth of time-space because it has to do with spirit and mind and with the intangibles such as love, faith, and fear. When we learn how to use this power, we shall be free of world problems just as Jesus was free of them. He overcame the world completely. Not even death had power over Him.

Speaking with authority hinges on our belief. We say

we have an idea, a heart's desire, something we want to do or to be or to possess. Well, where did that idea come from? It is a living entity, we now know. Both science and religion say that those big ideas come from God. Dr. Strömberg's book "The Soul of the Universe," explains this so clearly that even I can understand it. Then if the *idea* comes from God, we have no trouble in believing that we have already received. The instant we let that thought into our mind, we have actually received it. The thought form may be compared to the electric field which will hold the idea there until fulfilled. Our job is to hold it steady, not to break it up in any way. The power will do the work. But holding it is up to our faith. That we must supply.

Then to obtain our heart's desire we must learn to speak the word, and speak it *with authority*. All guesswork can be put aside. We can say: "God has given me this idea and so I have received. Now let it become manifest (the Word become flesh), and come to me, complete and whole."

We have talked about our ideas as being living people, little entities who go out into the world and bring back to us according to their kind. We added two other ideas to that: to put a song in the heart of them, and wings on them like the wings of a bird—two wings, purpose and attitude.

Now let's add another idea to that: *put a net in their hands.*

Nets are for catching things. That is what we want. We are going to send our big idea out into the world and instruct it to catch all the other ideas and things it needs to complete our big plan. We will send it out into unlimited space. Beyond this world? Yes, if necessary. Clear to God and back.

Are we talking nonsense? No, and here is but one example from life to show how it actually works.

Sir Alexander Fleming, who died at the age of

seventy-three, left a great legacy to mankind. He is the man who gave penicillin to the world. How did he discover it? The newspapers described him as "a giant of history, this gentle, reflective, blue-eyed Scot whom destiny made a witness to a magnificent accident—and endowed with the vision to perceive its import. The accident was the landing of an airborne shred of the mold *Penicillium notatum* on a culture of murderous staphylococci, in a London hospital laboratory in 1928. Observing destruction of the bacteria, Dr. Fleming isolated the mold and began to grow it."

This was the first of the antibiotics now used in the treatment of more than a hundred diseases—dedicated to humanity, with no profit to himself. No wonder "his death was mourned around the world." The great doctor was gone, but he left his light on.

Did he do all that himself? Note again the account: "destiny made a witness to a magnificent accident—" The shred of mold landed just where he could see it, and it came to a man here on earth who would understand the importance of what he was seeing. God at work. Here in Pasadena I have a friend, formerly a British subject, who was a trained nurse and often worked in the hospital in London where the great Dr. Fleming labored for mankind. She cannot speak of that great soul without tears in her eyes. He was a "love" person. *The desire of his heart was to help people.*

Someone may say: "He was an educated man and got a good start in the world. But I am poor." Look at another example:

Johns Hopkins was taken out of school at the age of twelve. His father, a Quaker, came to believe that owning slaves was spiritually wrong, and freed them. This so greatly impoverished the family that young Johns had to go to work.

The boy went to Baltimore and began. He became a millionaire merchant and railroad man. He set up a university and hospital, and in his will left seven million dollars to carry out his wishes. That was in 1874, and today all the world knows about Johns Hopkins University and Johns Hopkins Hospital.

Can we reasonably doubt that Johns Hopkins did his work, that he created his fortune, through the powers God had given him, that he was well aware of those powers, and used them consciously and with gratitude? If you walk into the Johns Hopkins Hospital today, you will see a large statue of Jesus Christ, which dwarfs the human figures that hourly pass by it. At the base of the statue is the inscription from the words of the Great Physician: "Come unto me, all ye that labour and are heavy laden, and I will give you rest."

The whole world is weary and heavily laden today with fears and problems, with conditions that man has created because man has worked contrary to the principles Jesus taught.

If great fame and lasting honor are desires of your heart, then get to work for humanity. If you want to do something so important that you will keep your own light shining when you go out, you must come under the law of love—so far under it that you will be willing to wash feet and feed sheep—with no profit to yourself.

God trusts His big ideas to the one who is so unafraid of life, so unselfish in service that he has time to listen to the voice of God, time to look at the fire in every bush around him.

If you have not yet selected a heart's desire big enough for you to be really excited about, may I suggest that you take on some problem facing the world today. First, lift yourself up, realizing who you are, what you are, why you are here on earth, and where you are going. You will then want to tell it to the world. You will want to spend the rest of your days trying to get others to go along with you. You will want to do this so wholeheartedly that you will do anything that is honorable which will awaken others to truth. You will have compassion on the weak, the slow to learn, the doubting, the fearful. You will find the natural way to wash feet and feed sheep. You will go among them, those who are looking in the wrong place for the security, the comfort for which they hunger. You will cry out: "This way! This way, brother. Look within your own being, and learn how to use the power God has given you!" Or you will say, "Behold what God has shown me," of some new miracle for the world.

If you start upon this path as a life work, you will find wings of angels lifting you up higher and higher in your desires and endeavors. From a certain height you will see that all is right with man and the world, that only learning and love are missing in order to create heaven on earth.

If you have the idea already, then start reminding yourself:

"God has given me a work to do
And all I need to see it through."

As troubles come (and they will), never look back. Look forward. Tell yourself every day of your life:
This is the best day of my life. Also: *This is the best day the world has ever seen.* For this is true.

Good is progressive. The whole world of men, as they rise in consciousness of the truth of their own nature, take you up higher with them, and you help them to rise. Every day the human race is a little further on the march toward God than it was the day before. All science proves this. So does religion. If you doubt it, take a brief look into recorded history.

Little more than a century ago in America, black men were chained and beaten as slaves. Little children worked in textile mills and got up at four o'clock in the morning to do so. In civilized, "Christian" England, sailors starved to death in the streets of London. Both children and women worked in the coal mines. Noblemen had their private hanging trees. Crime, death, and cruelty were so prevalent that Samuel Pepys listed them frequently in his famous diary as common occurrences.

Any way you look at it, today is the best day of your life and the best day the world has ever seen. Do not fear tomorrow. Speak with authority for a better tomorrow.

The great changes from the past days to these have all come about through the effort of love at work, individuals who cared enough to wash feet and feed sheep on the level they selected to serve. Their light is still burning.

Are you only an employee in a vast organization? You are not alone. A lead man in such an organization tells me that he and his men "sit around and talk about God and wonder just what Jesus was really talking about," as a means of opening their minds to new ideas.

Let your thoughts go out, let your ideas soar with a net, and they will wing their way back to you with new thoughts and ideas that will help you. Just thinking about the accomplishments of others will stir your own thoughts, if you will make a practice of it. Here are some thought stimulators:

In January, 1955, newspapers carried the story about "Nuclear Planes Seen in 1985 by Scientists," and gave a vivid picture of what we can expect by that year. Passenger airlines will be flying at 2000 miles an hour at altitudes of about fifteen miles. These are not daydreams. They are plans in the minds and on the drawing boards of hard-headed engineers and scientists, people who use facts. But their original ideas all came to them from God. Can anyone doubt it?

Here is another instance:

In the same newspaper from which I clipped the

127

above story there appeared another article concerning the "sun civilization" that is nearing as man harnesses light. A group of University of California scientists at Berkeley carried on experiments, headed by Dr. Daniel L. Arnon. They announced they had "harnessed sunlight to create sugar and starch out of water and carbon dioxide in the absence of green plants." This was news, indeed, for the world—it never had been done before. The meaning of it all is that the possibility of *inexhaustible food* supplies and *inexhaustible power* is now in sight for man.

Did not those scientists, through their own heart's desire to get answers to their scientific questions, tune in to and receive truths?

If you have a big idea, there are people all around you who are ready, willing, and able to help you. There are organizations of men, money, and skill ready to help. Into such organizations people everywhere are gladly pouring their money, for never before in the history of man has there been such a concerted effort to create a better world for all men. Many are helping to finance schools and other institutions for that very purpose, to help develop leaders for today and tomorrow. For example:

Methodist colleges and universities received a total of nearly $600,000,000 in special gifts during one year (1969). This was not taxes, demanded and paid. This was *love at work*. The heart's desire of a great many people is to help others in just such a way.

If your heart's desire has to do with religion as a way of life and you want to do research work, then the world is waiting for you. Everywhere people are turning to religion as a means of solving everyday problems and of giving meaning to all life. In England a movement investigates and reports on the many miraculous spiritual healings that are taking place there. The Church of England is in charge, calling in many of high authority to help.

Are the affirmations, speaking the word, really as powerful as we have hoped and discussed throughout this book? Those miracles taking place in England have come through the power of the word and those who know how to use the power. Then we have the authority of the Bible for our statements and our hope. The Religious Research Foundation has said, "We find that prayers of affirmation and objective visualization are most effective."

Charles Fillmore, cofounder of the Unity School of Christianity, said, "Words charged with power and intelligence increase with use, while material things decrease." It is true, and one spiritual leader whom I know quite well has had remarkable success with the method of making one affirmation one hundred times when he sets out to do a given work.

"All my desires, both big and small,
God hears and answers all."

To say this is to say it is so. Prayers are asking. Affirmations are saying it is already so.

The greatest help we can have in speaking our word with authority, it seems to me, is to keep in mind our overall view of man, his nature, the purpose of his life, and the powers God has given him. A theory of life which answers these questions gives purpose and plan to all the rest of life, including our individual and immediate problems. Besides that, it explains our desire to fulfill our urges and needs.

What is the purpose of the Power of our Word as God has given it to us? In answer to desire, long-continued prayer, meditations, and seeking, it has come to me so repeatedly through the past years that I no longer ask. The answer is always the same:

To teach man how to live forever.

That answer I accept. It gives me more peace than anything else that ever has come to me in all my life. No matter what happens today, what problems go unsolved, what the world is thinking, or who is threatening whom with what, I need not hurry, worry, fuss, or fret. What if I do fail time after time in working with the spiritual laws? I still have time to try again. What if atomic warfare does come? What if I grow old or sicken and die? What indeed? I shall still be alive. For I *am* life. I cannot die. I can only change form, go from school to school, learning, always learning. I never can be where God is not, never outside His love and care. Why should I worry? I don't.

Earth is a very small place, a tiny grain of sand. I say with Lord Jesus that in my Father's house—scheme of things—there are many worlds. Worlds without end. I am a Word of God and am important to Him. I know very little. I have not gone very far since He spoke me into existence. But I am headed right. I am moving. Every thought I direct toward God takes me further forward. Every question I ask, every effort I make to learn, to do, to be more, builds my soul for all eternity. When I do go from earth I shall take my personality, my memories, all I have learned to date, with me.

I have no fear, no regret, no hesitation. *For I know that I was made to last forever.*

And so were you, my friend.

The Consciousness of a New Earth

Seventeen years and four books later . . . a report on the steadily increasing conscious use of the power of the Word . . . by individuals, by two or more, by science.

Thou shalt also decree a thing, and it shall be established unto thee (Job 22:28 [A.V.]).

When James A. Decker, Unity's senior editor, arranged for the publication of this book as a serial in UNITY Magazine, and later as a hardcover book, I asked permission to add some new material for the new edition. Then I set to work on my years of accumulated material concerning the conscious use of the power of the Word to try to make the best selection possible for these four new chapters, and to try to help the reader a little further along in his search for truth.

This book was first published in 1955 by Dodd, Mead & Company. At the time of publication a reviewer said of it: "Ahead of its time and will not be as popular as the author's three previous books."

He was right. It did not sell as well as "Change Your Life through Prayer" and the other two of the trilogy that followed it. But it brought some of the most intelligent, searching, questioning, approving letters I ever received from my readers. And through the years, it has continued to bring astonishing reports, a sharing with me of experiences of others. These contacts included scientists, ministers, lawyers, doctors, and writers in this field.

More than any of my other books, it seems to me, *How to Use the Power of Your Word* points the way to tomorrow's better world. It tunes in on what is coming. The letters mentioned, plus stimulating conversations with fearless and forward-looking people, greatly encouraged me to continue research, record the outcome of work with my students, and set up a method of teaching that others can use.

Need has a way of catching up with those ideas and things that come out ahead of their time. It took a few years for people to accept the automobile and a much longer time for popular acceptance of the airplane. Today modern science shows an all-time high interest in some of the old ideas of the Bible as to the powers of man, the so-called miracles of Jesus, and the mysterious and mystic experiences of modern man.

Since this book was first published a great deal of water has gone under the bridge of time, and a good many bridges (ideas once held to be true but now discarded) have been washed away by the world's increasing consciousness of Truth. And so much has been taking place in our individual lives and affairs the past seventeen years, that I felt a report was necessary.

In preparation for writing this new material, I read this book through several times, as well as the three that preceded it, four that followed it, some of my personal diary that I have kept for years, and many of the case histories in my files. This was to find the growing trend—where we were, where we are, and in which way we are headed. After months of all this checking and note-making, the task looked hopeless. What I had was a new book in the making, and room for only four short chapters to add to this one.

After all that searching and comparing, I would not change a word of the first eight chapters of this book because it has to do with the *creative principle* of the Word, and principles do not change. But oh, what a lot of changes in our world affairs have taken place in these past seventeen years! Every major one had many proofs of the conscious use of the power of the Word.

Historians may recall the many worldwide events and changes in nations, laws, the down-dip in morals and human behavior, politics, wars, customs, and discoveries of this era, and think of them as influencing the minds and outlook of people. This is true, of course. But there is the other side of the coin: the great events, people struggling to become free as a nation, the hundreds of thousands of new inventions and processes that add good to the world, because of the events, were the *results of millions of spoken words;* never ceasing to try for new things, new ideas, fulfilling new desires. For one example, no one can estimate the number of words (prayers) that were sent out for the success and safety of the men on the first moon trip.

All within a few years the once "impossible" has become commonplace, and man is now headed for other planets because he has first gone there in *desire, decision, picturing with his mind,* and has *spoken the powerful words: "We can!"* It was about twenty years ago that the scientists began to say, "We will put men on the moon by 1985." Then it was "by 1970." As the world knows, it was on July 20, 1969 that Neil Armstrong and Edwin Aldrin actually walked on the moon, while millions watched by television around the world. The word of the thousands of people involved in the moon project did not return unto them void, but accomplished what they had said they could do. And that is but one part of the great new consciousness of this space age.

All of these world events are rapidly taking man into that new heaven and new earth which he has longed for since he began to wonder, to think, and to dream of something bigger, something better, something more than he had before. Today the number of individuals

133

who are consciously using the power of their Word for definite results, and keeping track of how they did it, has increased beyond counting. We have space here for listing only a few instances that have come under my personal witnessing.

In my own work, I have continued to create new *Logos*, or "Word people," to help my students, and for my own studies. Starting with A for *alcoholics*, they now run through the alphabet to Z for *greater zest in living.* For example: one alcoholic took a stand with his conscience and free will, used Word people for help with his thoughts which led to emotions and acts. He sent out Word servants of courage for himself, to avoid harming others, and to avoid meeting people who would want him to drink. He envisioned a little Word man I had thought up for him and named Sober Sam. "Sober Sam will keep me sober just for today," he would say, and he believed it. After he was healed he came to realize that with God's help, wisdom, and love, he could simply use the power of his Word direct. But he "hung on" to Sober Sam to help him in other parts of his life and work.

When the alcoholic believes that his Word companion who is with him hourly, daily, and knows him well, still loves him, he starts to feel that he is worthy of love. He then starts to love himself and sees that his drinking was actually a search for God, a soul-comforting that nothing else had brought. When the disturbed, searching person finds love for himself he becomes a new person. Love builds faith. The former alcoholic puts his faith to work. I hold that the greatest need in any one's life is the assurance that God does exist, and that God loves him, *no matter what.* Many of my students have come to accept and daily speak the word of Truth: *God does love me, no matter what!* This powerful word creates a whole new consciousness and outlook for them. Then the spiritual law, "As he thinketh in his heart, so is he," takes over.

Many have used the little Word people to help them stop smoking cigarettes. Different students give their Word people names that please them. Some have become so adept at the "game" of this psychological practice that they overcome a great deal of loneliness. This finally leads the student to the practice of the presence of God. One cigarette smoker told me, "I am quite aware of the fact that my Word partner stops people from offering me a cigarette." A woman who lived alone and had come to dread going home nights after work used a Word companion we called Happy Hannah. She overcame the feeling of loneliness and became a friend to others.

The student using the power of his Word soon learns to use the *power of picturing*, seeing ahead, the good he desires. This is of course one of the powers Jesus used. But along with all his Word companion practice, the student must also learn the laws of love and try to live within them, because what he actually is working with is the creative power of God. And God is love.

Naturally, we work with the spiritual laws from the level of our present understanding. But as long as we have the key that turns the lock, they work for us. For example, some people in using the power of their Word, and the Word people, visualize the person Jesus. People who have all their lives belonged to a fundamentalist church find it hard to think of God as all-love. One woman, daughter of a minister, said: "To think of facing God scares me sick; but I know Jesus is my friend and savior. He will stand between me and the wrath of God."

There was small use at that time to try to get her to think of God as Creator, all-love. Her consciousness was full of ideas of a God of wrath and punishment. The devil was very real to her, always lurking about to get her into trouble. She came through an ordeal by constantly picturing the form of Jesus, the Man near her when she needed help. It was some years before she expanded her consciousness and used the power of her Word directly and swiftly to say: "God has given me the power to help myself. Jesus has taught me to use it directly. So I now speak the word for (the need or problem at hand)." This practice eliminated her fears. She no longer felt trapped by life and circumstances. She no longer needed to hate and fear the devil as a person tempting her to "sin and evil." Since hate is a defense against fear, she no longer believed in a personal devil, and could overcome both hate and fear. Later still, she accepted the fact that she had free will, natural desires, emotions, and that her job was not to hate a devil, but to learn soul (self)-control.

Another woman who had joined a church that prohibits the use of tea or coffee to its members could not at first break the habit. "I drink coffee all day long," she said, "and I cannot become a final member until I give it up."

Searching for a starting place for the student, I tied in her faith in tithing. She had a very high faith that her tithing did prosper her; that Jesus, the Person, prospered her. Finally I said, "Since Jesus can, will, and does prosper you when you tithe, He can and will take away all desire for coffee if you ask Him to do so, and accept the fact that He can." She took a copy of this book home with her and was soon free from the coffee habit. She then went on to a direct use of her Word. But I must report that not all do so. Many people, it appears, are not yet ready to accept responsibility for their thoughts, feelings, words, and actions.

The practice of using the power of the Word for others at a distance is increasing. A woman whom I have never met, living in New York City, wrote that she knew when I was "holding her up in prayer." She explained that "suddenly there is a warmth in this bare, ugly, cold room. It is as if an electric heater had been turned on." This so greatly increased her faith that she worked with the power of her Word and "talked herself out of that miserable room" into one more worthy of a child of God. This is but one of many cases of people at a distance feeling a warmth, or of being made aware in some other manner that prayers were being said for them. Some of these examples included servicemen away at war.

My files include cases of instant healings through use of the power of the Word. In several other cases, people who had "gone out of their body" in an accident or illness, and who did not want to pass on and felt that it was not time for them to do so, discovered that they had the power to get back into the body. These facts are of tremendous importance in our studies of the whole man. Such authorities as Bible scholar Thomas Troward and scientist A. Cressy Morrison tell us how and why we are able to think, feel, and use *the power of imagination* in the state called death. I believe that there is no such thing as death for the human soul, the Self, the personality, the entity. I agree with those authorities who say that we are able to think, imagine, picture, and so *mentally speak the Word.*

When I remember that Jesus taught, "Be it done for you as you have believed," and that He set no limit on the operation of this believe-receive law, new possibilities of using the power of the Word open up before us for here and hereafter. Also, a careful study of the words and actions of Jesus long before the crucifixion leads me to believe that He knew He could use the power of His Word to "build it [the temple] in three days," meaning His own body.

The power of the Word might rest in the soul itself. I have experimented with this power during sleep and dreams, and have a growing file on my own experiences and those of others. The late Dr. David Seabury used to tell us in class how he ordered the kind of dream he wanted to have, and how and why it turned out that way. Since I have given several of my word-dream experiences in my book "Beyond the Darkness," we need not take space for them here. The point is: here is a power open to all, and surely it is one of the keys to a better tomorrow. To be able to speak the Word for answers to problems to come in dreams has been proved by many, and such accounts have had wide circulation. Scientists have used the method for their own work.

Much of my research time on points of Truth—what can be done to set man free—is spent learning sequences, the law of cause and effect, sowing and reaping, which Jesus taught as unbreakable spiritual laws. Our need is twofold: to learn how to set the causes into motion with our Word, and to trace results, both wanted and unwanted, back to the originating cause. So I think it is important to report on the following.

Sociologists cite many cases of four or more generations in a family of feeble-minded, poverty-stricken families. The Bible says that the "infirmity of the father," the mistakes, will be visited "upon the children to the third and fourth generation." What we often overlook is that children grow up to imitate what they hear and see around them; especially do they imitate their parents. "If you house with a cripple you will learn to limp," says the proverb. Modern doctors have found that children hump over or imitate other physical defects of their parents or adults in the home, with no physical cause of their own to cause a defect.

It works the other way around, too. Great good has been and is being achieved in moral, mental, and spiritual growth in families. Good genes are passed on through inheritance and produce superior children. The purposely planned and carried out environment of hope, faith, love, courage, moral, and mental discipline taught with powerful words builds the child's consciousness and frees him from the problems of failure's child.

For years I have known a wonderful couple, both outstanding people. The husband is a professional man, the wife (who once studied with me) is a natural teacher of children. She gave up teaching school to teach their three daughters. All three girls won awards in school and were outstanding students. Today those three daughters have given the parents nine grandchildren. All the grandchildren are astonishing in their intelligence, grasp of life, total ideas of their worth and abilities. They are classified as "greatly talented," some as geniuses. In a modern I.Q. test given at school some of these children "run off the chart," being superior to any test yet devised for measuring the whole child.

Discounting the value of such tests, we still must see that here is a case of improving human beings. How was it accomplished? I think the outstanding factor is the *religious feelings* of the grandparents, and the tremendous amount of talented time both parents took to train the children, as well as the good work they continue with their grandchildren. Those grandchildren are well aware of the existence of the power of their Word as a force that all people eventually will use readily. The school-age children of the family are observing the working out of spiritual laws in the world around them. With a few generations of highly moral, spiritual, mentally inquiring, honest, happy, loving, purposeful people, man would build a better world.

The second part of bridging the gap from the first part of this book to these final new chapters has to do with the increase of conscious use of the power of the Word for a definite and named purpose, by "two or more gathered together."

Today there are many prayer and spoken-word teams. They work to increase their own and the faith of others, before they speak the Word for themselves or others. I have found that a man and woman working together as spiritual prayer partners often are more successful than two women or two men partners. The reason, I think, is that men being positive and women being negative in electrical powers, form the necessary circuit for the creative power to work through them. I have written a good deal about this method of using the power of the Word, but there is no space for it here. The reader is advised to make his own experiments.

Another indication of the increase in the conscious and purposeful use of the power of the Word is found in the increased number of retreats held throughout the world, and especially in America. There is also an increase in the number attending such retreats, and the spiritual understanding of those conducting and attending is of tremendous importance. These dedicated and determined-to-learn people are, through their prayers, meditations, invocations, affirmations, songs, workshops, and acting-out in plays, adding good to the soul of the universe. Dr. Strömberg in his book shows how this is true and the value of it. We now know that the more good we add to the world soul, the easier it will become for others to learn and advance in the use of the power of their Word.

More than one thousand new folders and letters came to my desk in 1971, telling me of the aims and works of new organizations in religious, self-help, psychological, political, and public-welfare groups. If some of these programs are, as a woman reported to me "wacky, and I'll never attend again," it is not to be wondered at or condemned. People start from the level of consciousness where they presently live. The fact that they are getting involved with others, trying to advance, is the important point. People getting to know people is good training, and some learning (often considerable) takes place. These groups are due to increase, according to present indications. Not all are religious but all have some central intention of human improvement, and that is love at work and therefore good.

Another reason that these retreat groups are increasing is that large numbers of people have left their traditional churches, where they feel that soul-searching and experimenting with newfound truth are being held back. The growing edge people are proving the truth given in the *ninety-first Psalm:* that the individual can go through, no matter what the group may be doing or failing to do. The falling or the failing ten thousand cannot bring down the individual who knows how to use the power God gave him, to stand, understand, survive, and grow.

But the most significant growth in the interest, research, and practice of the individual use of the power of the Word is being made by scientists. For the first time in history, science and religion are working together in new ways to help man understand himself, and so understand others. He is learning facts about his own inner powers to control conditions of his body, mind, and spirit. He is learning that he can heal himself by an act of his mind and spirit. He is learning how to cooperate with the Intelligence that rules the universe. We have space here for only one reference, to Dr. Elmer Green of the Menninger Foundation in Topeka, Kansas. I report here from an article by Ralph Rhea, which appeared in UNITY Magazine in November-December of 1971:

Dr. Green and his wife Alyce, working in the psychobiology laboratory at Menninger, have used a machine that identifies brain waves of the patient. Through this they have helped their patients in a project they call "voluntary control." Summed up, they have proved that the patient can, through an act of his mind, send the blood out of his head, where it is causing a migraine, down to the hands, or send blood to the feet when they are cold. The whole project shows that man does have the power of his Word to help control the processes of his body. Since the work will go on, undoubtedly it will become normal procedure in teaching people about emotions, brain waves, their health, and their power to help themselves.

Such experiments are a way of teaching the patient how to use the power of his Word. They are also proving that the power of prayer is real. Emerson said, nearly a hundred years ago, "Our prayers to ourselves are always answered."

Some religionists may object to mechanical aids to the power of prayer and the spoken Word, but I find no fault with any aid to increase the consciousness of one's powers, and to heal any kind of suffering real or imaginary, mental, physical, or spiritual. To be made whole is the objective. And didn't Jesus put mud on the eyes of the blind man and tell him to go bathe in the river, so that he could see? Jesus knew that some people must have a "sign" or physical proof before they can accept a healing through faith, prayer, and the spoken Word.

To become whole is our goal. When we are whole we can help others to become whole. Paul was not entirely a whole person when he set out to persecute the Christians. He had a spiritual blind spot, and he was stricken physically blind because of that. Today we know that what we hold in mind, in spirit, intents, and purposes, in our emotions, our soul Self, if not checked will in time manifest in our physical body, our mental health, and our affairs. It works both ways. If we continue to believe in the use of the power of our Word, we will eventually use it . . . and effectively.

In reporting the increased use of the power of the Word for good, we should mention the fact that a great deal of goodwill is currently being engendered by a common use of the power of the Word without much thought or knowledge of what the words accomplish. I refer to our current custom of saying to everyone, "Now have a good day!" The checker at the grocery store, the boy who wheels my groceries out to my car, the man who picks up the laundry, the attendant who services my automobile, all tell me to "have a good day." And recently, after a session with my teeth, my dentist said to me rather absentmindedly, "Have a good day, Mrs. Mann."

"Why, Doctor," I said, "don't you know that every day I have is better than the day before? Of course *I'll* have a good day. *You* have a good day, Doctor!"

The dentist, a most intelligent man, was too startled to answer, such is the power of habit. I had broken the expected routine. I was supposed to say "Thank you" and just go on. But I am a vocal person and given to saying what I think. And I think that use of this friendly little greeting—"Have a good day"—ought to reach epidemic proportions. It is a good use of the power of the Word at a very common level. It spreads to other levels of thinking. Yesterday I saw on the rear bumper of an automobile a sign in bright yellow letters: *The P.O.W.s never have a good day.* To think of prisoners of war *not* having a good day is to go up into the area of the consciousness of love. And I'm all for it.

Not everyone is having a good day, or even a good night's sleep, not even in these United States, still said to be the wealthiest and freest nation on earth. Many think this nation will fall, as did Rome. Some think we are coming to the end of the human race—extinction. They cite all of the thirty-six classic examples of what is wrong. Many have lost the joy of living, have lost sight of the very purpose of man's being on earth.

We do not need to lose hope.

Actually, we are headed for the greatest age of man the world has yet seen. The turmoil of today is due to the fact that Jesus, the Christ-consciousness Man, used the power of His Word to set up the Truth movement.

He already had disposed of many old thoughts and beliefs with His Word: "You have heard that it was said . . . but I say to you—." The Sermon on the Mount was almost pure "new thought" for the human race at that time—so new that no one has yet lived up to all of it fully.

There is a way to live with today's turmoil, without hurting or getting hurt. It has to do with the right use of the power of the Word. We need to remember daily that right now we are creating a new heaven and a new earth.

The more facts we have about a given problem or condition, the better we can handle it. We are in need of understanding the fact that we are in the age of Truth. We need to think more about how it began and what it means to us today and what it has to do with the use of our power of the Word.

New Thought,
a Timeless Persuasion

How Jesus started the Truth movement with the Power of His Word . . . the age of Truth . . . the Bible of Man . . . a world library.

Then I saw a new heaven and a new earth (Rev. 21:1).

Thy will be done,
On earth, as it is in heaven (Matt. 6:10).

In his great book "Spirits in Rebellion," Charles S. Braden traces the Truth or New Thought movement back about a hundred years. His book is listed as "the story of the beginnings and growth of New Thought and kindred American metaphysical healing movements." It is a masterpiece of historical reporting.

It is true that New Thought and kindred movements are only about a hundred years old. But the Truth movement is nearly two thousand years old. In order to see where we, the people of the world, stand today, and in which way we are headed, we should look back to the beginning of the age of truth.

History shows how Jesus, the Christ-consciousness Man, started the New Thought and Truth movement. In John 8:32, Jesus says, "You will know the truth, and the truth will make you free." From the first, Jesus was working for the new man, the new heaven and the new earth. He was working for the kind of freedom for all men that He had found, developed, and used for Himself. He did this through knowledge of and obedience to certain spiritual laws. The total of these laws, Jesus called Truth.

In John 14:12 Jesus speaks the word for our day and apparently for all of our tomorrows, until the fullness of His Word has been accomplished. He said, "He who believes in me will also do the works that I do; and greater works than these will he do." Then Jesus added a qualifying clause which we seldom see quoted, but which I believe is the key to the whole matter: "because I go to the Father."

Going further, in John 14:16 Jesus makes His great promise which we know was kept: "And I will pray the Father, and he will give you another Counselor, to be with you for ever." This plainly includes our day and our tomorrow.

In John 14:17, Jesus spells out His meaning: "even the Spirit of Truth." These words spoken to His disciples just before the crucifixion were to assure them that help would come to them after He had gone. For our purpose here, we should cite John 14:25, where Jesus again speaks that the "Counselor, the Holy Spirit, whom the Father will send in my name, he will teach you all things, and bring to your remembrance all that I have said to you." Today some of the greatest thinkers in the world are researching the meaning of the teachings of Jesus.

In His use of the power of the Word (which is a masculine, mental, and projective power), Jesus impregnated the world Soul (which is a feminine, spiritual, and receptive power) with the Spirit of Truth. Jesus said that "he will teach you all things," which indicates that the Spirit of Truth also is a masculine, mental, and projective power. This impregnation gave birth to the age of Truth. While an age in the Bible is considered to be two thousand years, it may actually be much longer.

This Spirit of Truth is to remain with man "for

ever." So it may be that while an age does end in two thousand years, the Spirit is timeless. In one place, Jesus says that heaven and earth will pass away but His words will not pass away. To sum up this thought, the Spirit of Truth is alive in the world Soul and always will be. With every new finding of truth, things change in accordance with the new truth.

Putting it all together, we see that Jesus used the power of His Word to set up a way of final safety, or salvation, for the people of the world . . . for the new age. We don't have to die and go to a heaven in the skies before we can be happy, live a life of complete freedom, joy, peace, creatively, in harmony with our environment, our Creator, ourself and each other. Heaven means a state of complete harmony. A new heaven and a new earth definitely are due. This new heaven, which first is built in the heart of man, will manifest or "be done on earth" as it is in that heaven in the heart. The peaceable kingdom of the Old Testament yet will be established on earth. In that day there will be "no more hurt" on earth.

But we need to look further. After Jesus had spoken the Word that invoked the Spirit of Truth into the world Soul, it began to stimulate the mind of men to exploring, questioning, searching for reality. It is the foundation on which modern science rests. Truth found out, accepted, and used always leads to freedom in some degree. Total truth, things as they are, fact found out, includes the will of God. This total truth will finally give man the same freedom that Jesus had.

We should remember that at the time of Jesus, the world was largely in slavery; people were in prisons of sickness, poverty, ignorance, fear, hatred, and desires for revenge as well as being in political prisons. They were bound by rituals, creeds, myths, superstitions, cruelties, and suffering beyond anything we have today. The storm that the spoken words of Jesus generated has been gathering momentum every hour since and is now breaking over the world in an ever-increasing rate of speed and fury. Every myth, mistake, ignorant belief, and outright lie that harms and holds back the progress of the human race must and will fall. That is why we have so much outer turmoil in the world today. Many do not want the truth revealed. Many are afraid of the loss of profits or something else they value, if truth continues to open up the mind of man. Religious beliefs and practices, theories once held by science, are all rapidly changing in the light of new truth, facts found out, things as they really are. This situation confuses many. Some people are so untaught that they cannot cope with modern life. Millions of illiterates cannot hope to compete with educated groups. Many of the educated few (said to be about 2% of the people of the world) see little hope for our many modern problems.

Truth is the key that turns the lock that sets man free from his many prisons.

The advanced student who cares to take the time to study the history of the progress of Truth will greatly enlarge his soul growth. For example: truth about the worth of a man, because he was created by God, brought in Magna Charta for the "common" men of England and protection from the King. Truth about the rights of the individual to political freedom brought on the American Revolution, our Constitution and Bill of Rights (which every schoolchild should know and every adult should read now and then). Lincoln, a deeply religious man, spoke the truth when he said, "No man is good enough to own another" in freeing the slaves. In general the great events of history that have led to greater freedom for man, whether political, economic, or physical, social or cultural, have come from a new vantage point of Truth.

The spirit of Love, which Jesus also spoke into the

world Soul, is a feminine quality. Hence man has two good parents: the stern, mental-masculine, exacting and projecting force of Truth, and the soft, nourishing, comforting and creating, protecting, regulating force of Love. Our Father God and Mother Nature continue to bring us up in the way we should go. In spite of good parents and all the help and protection they give, the individual can fail on earth in his own life if he tries to live outside the spiritual laws. He has free will. He can use it to lead him to heaven—all harmony—or to hell— inharmony, a disturbance of body, mind, and spirit.

Every one of the prayers, words, and thoughts of Jesus have become a part of the world Soul and every one of these forces influences our life today. Just so, every word of man becomes a part of the world Soul and also influences the words of all men. When words of love, truth, and harmony outweigh words of inharmony, falsehood, and destruction, we will build that new heaven of harmony in the heart of man—and with it, he will build a new earth.

That is what the Truth movement is all about: learning and teaching the truth that frees. No single group in the Christian churches has done more to keep the words of Truth alive in the mind of man than has Unity School of Christianity during the past eighty years. For many years, the words "You will know the truth, and the truth will make you free," appeared on Unity publications. Only God knows how many millions of people have been inspired by those words. People in sick beds, in prisons, in lonely rooms, and on crowded subways, as well as in churches, study centers, and happy homes have been helped by those words.

Today, there is in the world Soul a quickening and ever-increasing search and demand for Truth, resulting in an ever-increasing demand for greater and greater freedom for the individual.

Many people are not ready yet to handle the freedom that they demand (and in many cases, the political freedom that has been granted). Others, able to handle freedom for themselves, cannot cope with those who can't. So we have a worldwide turmoil that touches in some degree every person in the world.

That is where we stand today in the age of Truth. But the good side of it is that millions are even now building a new heaven in their hearts and looking forward to a better world for all. Many are asking what more can be done to bring in greater and greater points of Truth—and so, more and more freedom for all mankind.

As I keep track of the rapid increase in the number of New Thought and Truth churches, the creation of many new truth-seeking organizations, plus the findings of modern science, my belief increases that we are close to a great new world of freedom for all.

Now I would like to share with the reader a few ideas about a work that I feel should be done:

I believe it is time for a new Bible.

By this, I hasten to add, I do not mean a new translation of the existing Holy Bible. I mean *an entirely new Bible*. My working title for it is "The Bible of Man." The Holy Bible is considered to be the Word of God, written down by divinely inspired men, accurate without a mistake.

To say I think we need a new Bible is in no way a criticism of the Holy Bible. Quite the opposite: every word in it should be kept for our age and all ages to come, as a guideline of thoughts, feelings, revelations of value to the ever-evolving soul of man. The Holy Bible is a history of the growth of the soul of man in his never-ending search for God and for answers to the question, "What is man that thou art mindful of him?"

The Holy Bible is the most remarkable library of literature of its kind in the world. It is the most revered Book by the greatest minds the world has yet produced. Without the Bible there could have been no civilization as we know it today. It has guided Europe for the past two thousand years. William Lyon Phelps said that "the Bible has been a greater influence on the course of English literature than all other forces put together." C. B. McAfee said: "The Bible is a book-making book. It is a literature which provokes literature." And it was Voltaire who said, "Books rule the world." Well, the Bible has ruled the world for the past two thousand years. The human race will never outgrow it.

So what kind of a Bible am I talking about, and what part will it play in helping the world of men go forward?

The oldest cry of men is, "What must we do to be saved?" This meant to be saved after death, and in the Christian religion, to be saved from the wrath of God, punishment for wrongdoing. For the new age, and the new needs of man, there should be an Age of Truth Bible, which I think of as the Bible of Man, written by men, no less inspired by the power of God than were the writers of the Holy Bible. The difference is that the Bible of Man will tell man how to be saved on earth . . . how to come free, now.

The Bible of Man, as I see it, would be a report on the two thousand years of man's search for God, his mistakes, his religious activities, both good and bad, since the Crucifixion. It would take in the rise of science, the search for truth, and would include those facts discovered by archaeology. In short, the essence or soul of all that man's search for Truth has revealed about the soul of man and his possibilities, plus his findings that prove the Bible to be true as written (or found not to be true as yet).

The Bible of Man would be a report on the growth of the mind, soul concepts, and works of man which have largely been inspired by religion. It should of course take in the findings of all men which point to the truth about what man is, where he came from, what his purpose is on earth, what is the highest, best thing he can do while on earth, and where he goes when he leaves earth. Within the bounds of truth, the Bible of Man would report on reincarnation, if it has been found to be a truth by the time the Bible of Man is put together.

I feel strongly that this new Bible should include man's mistakes in trying to lead what he felt was a religious life . . . for example, the Inquisition, the religious wars, the burning of witches. But also it should include a report on what man did right by holding to the tenets of religion as he understood it. Surely it should include mention of great religious reforms and other reforms, such as reforms for prisons, etc., which resulted from individuals trying to lead a Godly life.

The teachings of Jesus never have been put together and tested by modern science, but I believe this will be done. People need two feet to walk on: faith and fact.

What should go in the Bible of Man is of course a question for the experts. I have merely voiced my own feelings. The experts exist in the world of science, religion, philosophy, and literature. These four foundation walls would support a mighty new Bible. I feel certain that the idea of a Bible of Man already exists in the hearts and minds of enough people to start a project that will not end until it has been brought into existence. In these days of computers that can add millions of times faster than a man can, and other mechanical aids, there is great hope that such an undertaking could be begun and completed as this century ends.

Along with this idea, I believe that we are even now in need of a great world library. In my thoughts I have called it the Truth and Freedom Library. This library should be a depository of books that have helped man to truth and freedom in every area of his life during the past two thousand years. Man needs to understand the greatness of the mind and soul within him . . . to stand taller, to reach up higher.

More than sixty years ago, Charles P. Steinmetz said: "Someday the scientists of the world will turn their laboratories over to the study of God and prayer and the spiritual forces . . . when this day comes the world will see more achievement in one generation than it has in the past four generations."

All of these thoughts and feelings of need are now part of the world Soul. I daily speak the Word for this new man, new age, to come in. And I daily speak the Word for a new Bible and that World Library of Truth and Freedom. For I am convinced that our struggle to pass laws, to try to change people through political changes, is doing more harm than good in many ways. We need to help people change their individual lives for the better through a knowledge and use of Truth that will set them free. When enough people have accomplished that, the laws will automatically change. Not force, but love and learning, are needed to build a better world.

Many people are frightened by the idea of learning to do the things Jesus did. "Why," they say, alarmed, "if ordinary people could use the power of the Word as Jesus did, then criminals and other evil-minded people can also use it! Jesus used it because He is divine, but we are not." Others say: "Such a power cannot be from God. It must be from the devil or some other evil force." And they want nothing to do with it.

Recently one of my good friends who likes to twit me about New Thought religion said: "Here you have been working in this field for years and not one of your followers has yet walked on water. Why do you keep on?"

I did not answer the good man. He has not yet developed his spiritual ears to that point of hearing truth and understanding. But you, dear reader, must have come to that place, or you would not have this book in your hands. So let me tell you why I keep on in this work.

It is because I believe with my whole heart that a new world is coming in, built on the teachings of Jesus and modern science. I want to do all I can to help bring it in. So let me tell you something of what I see about this "new earth."

Before you start to read the next chapter, I ask you to remember as you read that Truth itself, being a holy servant of God, will drive everything unlike itself before it to make way for the age of freedom to come in. Only the advanced and advancing, or desiring-to-advance, individuals see ahead, in truth. For example, Morrison, in his book "Man Does Not Stand Alone," said:

"The early Greeks knew that the earth was a sphere, but it took two thousand years to convince men that this fact is true. New ideas encounter opposition, ridicule, and abuse, but truth survives and is verified."

About fifty years ago, some psychiatrists were saying that to believe in God was a sign of mental illness; that God is a myth. Truth has caught up with that idea. Today, the greatest psychiatrists are saying (as Jung believed) that not believing in God is a sign of mental illness.

There always are great ideas (insights) and books ahead of their day. Dr. J. B. Rhine's book "The Reach of the Mind," was thought not to be "scientific" by some scientists. Dr. Rhine has had a struggle to get scientific acceptance of his work. But today, he is widely accepted.

Jesus was two thousand years ahead of His time. But once a part of Truth comes into the world Soul, it is there to stay. It finally penetrates many minds ready to receive it. I think that by tomorrow, or the day after, millions will accept the fact that Jesus was using a natural power, open to all, when He did the works now rated as "miracles."

Learning to Be a Love Person

For to him who has will more be given, and he will have abundance; but from him who has not, even what he has will be taken away (Matt. 13:12).

Jesus expected a new heaven on earth. He said, "I came that they may have life, and have it abundantly." His total teachings, ministry, and works showed that this could come about, bring in the age of freedom, under the law of cause and effect, sowing and reaping. The Bible verse above has puzzled many, who think that it would be unfair to take away what a man has. But it seems clear that Jesus was saying that whatever a man holds in his consciousness will manifest in his life and affairs. Even if he has inherited a fortune but has only poverty in his consciousness, he will, by his own consciousness, draw the events that will take the fortune away from him. These are some of the truths that the majority of people will have to learn before the age of freedom can come in fully. Of course, freedom for individuals will come as they learn the truths that will set them free.

The new earth, long called "heaven on earth," will become a reality when enough people (both Christian and nonChristian) accept the fact that they really can do the works Jesus did, and greater works. In that day of freedom all tears and fears will be wiped away. The great good coming in that tomorrow will include health for everyone. Sickness as we now know it will have passed from the earth. We will not be interested in heart transplants, for example, because we will have learned how to keep the heart of each individual in good working order, his whole life through. There will be no painful surgical operations. Physicians will heal as Jesus did, directly by the power of the Word.

In the age of freedom, there will be no mental illness. Today we have millions of so-called mentally ill people. I believe many of them are actually so spiritually sick, so confused about life and the powers of man, about how to maintain themselves on earth, that they have lost their way as normal human beings. Tomorrow they will know the way. There will be no need and no way to hide from life. Mentally ill patients will not be given powerful drugs to quiet them down. They will be daily given facets or doses of Truth until they learn—and then there will be no mental illness at all. Children will be taught their own powers and will be afraid of nothing. There will be no need, no occasion for loneliness, no welfare systems, no prison or jails, and few if any divorces.

The new day, the new man, the new earth will be a coordinated and smoothly running order of events for all concerned. There will be no hungry, unfed people. Every child will receive a good education, and travel around the world to learn geography and history, to meet the peoples of the world, as part of his education and to find his place and work in the world. Trips to other planets will be as common as air flights around the world are today, and far easier, with no noise and no pollution.

Food for all, leisure, pleasure, happiness, health, learning, the joy of living and exploring—how will all this good come about?

There will be several stages of development. First, the greatly expanded moral consciousness of man, along with modern science, will produce the energy needed, so cheaply that earth will become a well-ordered paradise. The knowledge of how to release that energy is already known and plans for working with it are now under way. The moral consciousness of man has so far outgrown the idea of war as a way to acquire good that war is doomed. The billions of dollars, the energy and time wasted on war will be invested in human betterment the world around. And the pain, frustration, unproductivity of those wounded in war, as well as the pollution and destruction, the immense cost of care, will have ended. Loss will be turned into productivity.

All this is coming much sooner than many are able to believe. Once all these problems are solved, the individual will have more time, inclination, and ability to study and to practice Truth, to set a goal of learning to do the things Jesus did.

With new knowledge and new freedoms increasing, thousands of individuals will start to learn how to use the atomic power that fills all space, which Jesus knew and used so freely and at will. Today we look at the results of the use Jesus made of atomic and electronic power as "miracles." Jesus used natural law and natural power. He is the only man so far who understood this natural power and the laws under which it operates. He said, "I have overcome the world." He had overcome the *world consciousness* of that day, which was bound by ideas of poverty, fear, sickness, mistakes that led to cruelty, greed, persecution, hostility, hate, and war. That same world consciousness is holding man back today. But it can be changed, because man can learn how to change. The good news is that many people are so highly evolved in moral goodness that they could quickly grasp the principles Jesus used and learn to use them.

Jesus was aware of a natural power within Himself that enabled Him to contact, direct, and control the power locked up in every atom on earth. Atoms are the building blocks of things that can be seen. Jesus used the power of His Word within Himself as His dominion, His authority to do His will with the atoms and electrons of the human body; to rearrange those atoms so that the leper's flesh instantly became clean. Jesus used the power to still the wind and waves of the sea, and to see at hand a harvest that was months away. He used this power to multiply the atoms in cooked fish and loaves of baked bread in a basket. He did it by calling on the free-flowing atoms to add themselves to the existing pattern: in short, to multiply.

Jesus is the only person yet who used His "dominion over all," the power which we are told in Genesis is common to all men. Jesus used that dominion over all to put life back into the dead Lazarus, to command life to return to the widow's son and to the young girl. He used it to change His own "dead" human flesh body into a new, shining body of atoms that was made of such high energy that those at the tomb described it as "light." He warned the others not to touch Him. Because they were in a flesh body, they were of a different vibration of energy. To have touched Him might well have harmed Him and themselves. Later Jesus developed a body which they could see, and which Thomas touched.

Jesus was in such command of the atomic power in things that He could change water to wine, hear and see at a distance in both time and space. He used it to pass through closed doors and walls.

The great fact is that Jesus said that you and I, all men, have this same power in potential, within. He used this power through or by "the Father within." (He said He did what He saw the Father do.) He said that any man could learn the spiritual laws and how to work within them to do what He had done—use the power God gave Him. That power has complete authority over things of the world, but man will have to learn the law of love and live within it before he can make the power of his Word work for him. Jesus spelled out the law of love in the two great commandments.

For nearly two thousand years the Christian world has worshiped Jesus from afar, as "the only begotten son of God," a divine Being who therefore had powers that no one else ever had or could have. They have not believed or have overlooked the truth, or have been unwilling to learn how to work, to pay the price of such use of atomic energy directed by the power of the Word.

Through these centuries good Christians have begged Jesus, the Christ-consciousness Man, to do for them what He taught that all men can do for themselves. After the first century or so Christians gave up healing in the church; it called for too much self-discipline. Today many Christians still use the piggyback method in seeking help: "Please pick me up, dear Jesus, and carry me along." They think of themselves as helpless. They look upon Jesus as the great and powerful Shepherd and of themselves as helpless little lambs. And such is the love of God that all who ask are helped, if they can believe. The unhappy fact is that this method does not build the ability of one to help himself.

Jesus called Himself "the son of man." Scientist Lecomte du Noüy says that Jesus is the pattern of what all men will be eventually. He thought that Jesus was a million years ahead of today's man. I do not agree with du Noüy's point of time. He makes no mention of New Thought or the Truth movement. He seems not to have known about groups of Christians who believe that man can learn to do the things Jesus did. So-called miracles are taking place over all the world today at the command of ordinary beings, who have faith in the power Jesus used, and enough love to have faith in themselves.

Before God could grant to man the use of such power over atoms, He had to have a way to keep man from using it wrongly and destroying himself and others. When we see what this method is and how it works, it puts us on our knees in awe, wonder, and gratitude for the greatness of God and the unfathomable depths of His love for man, His child, His created being, who already is only a little lower than the angels and is destined to become as a god.

With the creative power within himself, man can become as a devil as well as a god. The margin of safety lies in the fact that man cannot use his power over the atoms until he has become a complete love person. (Man must do what he sees the Father doing.) Man is a child of God, but he has not yet reached his spiritual maturity as a Son of God until he has become a love person. Whenever he learns to live within the law of love, man will break through to the kind of freedom Jesus knew and used.

Many psychologists and psychiatrists say that for any one to want good instantly is infantile and unrealistic. I see their point of reasoning but cannot agree with them. They are judging after appearances and past experience. But "experience is not bound by precedent."

I think the infant may come inwardly equipped with a desire for instant satisfaction, so that he will work during his lifetime on earth to learn how to accomplish at will, as Jesus did. I think earth is a school where man is sent to learn how to use his free will in such a way that he harms no one, not even himself. To do this, he must learn to live within the law of love, which will take him on into the "instant" age.

All infants want to experience pleasure and avoid pain, and so do all grown-ups. If the growing child is allowed to refuse to accept the responsibility of his free-will acts, thoughts, and desires, he will remain a spiritual infant, not a love person. Such a spiritual infant will not be able to use the power of his Word in the way that Jesus did. It requires the highest state of spiritual maturity to do that.

Jesus showed that the use of the power is foolproof. Only people of love can use it. Jesus withered the fig tree. He could also wither the film over the eyes of the blind. But even so, the creative power must be of love, or the atoms will not obey the command. We have a history of black magic. Those who try to use it find that it rebounds on them and destroys them. Such people have been known to destroy themselves, in expiation of their sense of guilt. We see this happening in lesser degree in people all around us; it accounts for much of the physical ill-health and use of drugs—the search and demand for a good not earned with good.

But the universe remains safe. God is not mocked. If man wants to learn how to do the things Jesus did, he will have to become the kind of love person Jesus was.

Today man uses the reverse of the creative law Jesus used. Man has gone to great pains, devoted time, work, dedication, and money to splitting the atom, breaking up a unit of energy, unraveling something that God, creative Intelligence, has put together solidly to last, and out of which things on earth are made. Scientists now know that if they can release the power in the atoms, man can build a paradise on earth, of things. All the material good we have been talking about will become a reality.

Is this only a beautiful but unrealistic dream? No. It is sheer reality, truth, things as they actually are. Let's look a little farther at some facts.

Modern science says that space is charged with energies (raw power) that would transform the earth if we knew how to release and control them. Sir Oliver Lodge said that a single cubic inch of ether—that space out there—contains energy enough to run a forty-horse-power engine for forty million years! Man has been going at this problem of power control on the lowest level, which is physical force. By using the higher level of work—his own thought and spiritual power to command that energy—he can do the things Jesus did.

And Jesus said, "greater works." Since there is now greater general information and knowledge of need in the world (and more people) than there were in Jesus' day, man will naturally do greater works with the power of his word than Jesus did. He will not stop at multiplying food and healing sick bodies. He will use it to travel to other planets.

Our need is to learn how to become the kind of love person Jesus was, to have the faith of God working through us. Then we can learn to direct the power in the atoms as they are without having to split them by force. Jesus said that a man could move a mountain, if he had enough faith to command the mountain to be removed and cast into the sea. But His whole ministry, teaching, demonstrating His use of the power, proved His point that *we cannot have faith until we first have love.* This may be why Jesus used the image of moving a mountain, because it takes that much love to create that much faith.

Jesus showed that any infraction of the law of love weakens our faith to that degree. In His two great commandments Jesus sums up the way of life that works—the state of consciousness man must achieve before he can use his authority over all (including atomic energy) to do the things that Jesus did.

Mind working without or against love is destructive. Working with and within love, it is creative. In nature the old notion of good and evil—two powers, one of them evil, a devil able to overcome God or good—is not so. Tomorrow we shall see that it is one and the same power at work. Evil cannot create; it can only destroy, in principle. But it is limited in the extent to which it can use the power to destroy, for evil of itself is not an entity or a reality. Evil is the wrong way to go about

162

trying to obtain a desired good. Error can destroy on the physical plane, as bombs. It can destroy on the mental plane, as evil thinking proves, as desire to harm others. It can destroy on the emotional, feeling plane, and literally drive people insane. It can destroy on the spiritual plane, as immoral people prove. But it cannot contact, command, or direct the intelligence and the energy in the atom and electron as Jesus did. This can be done only under love. (The sheep know the voice of the good shepherd, and follow him.) Which brings us back to the oldest philosophy, which says that the universe is moral. Emerson and others have had much to say about this.

Love sent out can bring back only love. By tomorrow, millions will have learned so to live within the law of love that they will be using the power within themselves to control and use at will, both the free atoms in space to create things and the bottled—up atoms, such as blindness, cancers, calcium deposits that cause arthritis. Food plants will develop fully and instantly for man; there will be no wait from seed to harvest. Men will plant ideas, picture seeds of what they need and want, and direct free-energy (atoms) to come and assemble themselves in the framework, just as today bees come and fill in the honeycomb man has provided in the hive.

God's plan for man is so foolproof that no one of us can break it. We simply cannot work miracles outside of the law of love. We are learning. We shall finally make it. *Then* we can use the power of our Word!

The joy and happiness that is coming for man on earth is beyond our present understanding. Sometimes, in the silence of the night, I can mentally hear what the music will be like. We will have the kind of joy Jesus the Christ had. "Order is heaven's first law." Jesus said He came to teach people "that they may have my joy fulfilled in themselves." We often hear the phrase "the joy of Christ," but few stop to ask what it means or to realize that there is a way for them to have the same kind of joy—by learning the law of order.

Webster says of joy that it is "the emotion excited by acquisition or expectation of good; gladness, delight." That describes the joy of Christ. He knew He had the power of His Word to do the works He did. He knew all men have that power and are destined to learn how to use it. He knew men were not lost, "feeble and frail," nor yet "worms of the dust," but children of God, Sons of God in the making. Jesus knew so much of His power and future, and the future of man, that He was not afraid to die. Though He suffered agonies on the cross, He knew He could overcome it finally, and He did. So shall we all live, after what we now call death. *Life is eternal!*

We all want to be happy, know joy. Yet today millions of individuals are living in hell on earth. They all want joy and happiness. History is filled with examples of the way of life that does not work. We are now in the age of Truth, and many are learning of their powers.

"Oh," someone may say, "we are not yet in that great day. What I want is a point where I can start to learn to improve my life, build my consciousness. How and where do I start?"

We will take this up in Chapter Twelve.

Others may be thinking: "But why should we want or need to learn to do the things Jesus did, and greater things? Why can't we just leave well enough alone and keep on as we are? True, we have a lot of problems now, but things are sure to improve with time. What do we need that we don't already have?"

Why should we want to learn ahead, and enter the age of freedom? Because it will be grimly necessary to go up higher in consciousness if we are to hold civilization together. Millions will have to learn how to "do more with less" as our modern creative genius, Buckminster Fuller, says. In fact, the history of the work activities of man show that his efforts have always been to do more with less, from hollowing out a log for water transportation to building an ocean liner.

Doing more with less, through the intelligent use of the power of the Word, is the hope of the world. And it is coming sooner than most of us realize. The runners-ahead do see, and some will yet do tremendous works in our day. We can all help this new age come in by speaking the Word daily for it, and trying to live so as to help to bring it in.

But right now, this day—what can we do now? Let us go into that.

Working for the Endless Horizon

*"Let the words of my mouth and the meditation
of my heart
be acceptable in thy sight,
O Lord . . ."*

—Psalms 19:14.

When people come to me for prayers and to talk about their problems, I ask them:

"Where does it hurt?"

"What would it take to make you happy?"

"What would you like to have changed?"

"What is it you want me to pray about?"

In recording their case histories I learn what they have been doing with life; what they have held in consciousness most of the time. Their histories clearly show me what kind of word servants they have been sending out. It shows me what they have recently been thinking, talking about, and listening to, more than fifty percent of the time. With this information on paper for study, I know where the student stands, and in which way he is headed. It is my purpose then to see that he is headed in the right direction in order to reach his goal, make his dreams come true, and achieve the happiness and success that so far seem to have eluded him. For this project he needs a road map, meaning a method of procedure in learning the truth that frees, how to live within the spiritual laws, and how to use the power of his word.

He also needs a good self-image, a good estimate of himself as to what he is. One of his assignments is to read some of the Psalms, including the one quoted at the head of this chapter.

We start with whether the student is happy or unhappy, what his goals are, and whether they are high enough. Every mentally-disturbed, neurotic, and prone-to-failure person I have ever worked with had a history of unhappiness. But many entirely sound people are also unhappy. Their unhappiness generally has to do with others, or present world conditions, or a threatening situation over which they feel they have no control.

The unexamined life is hardly worth the living. As we work along the student takes self-evaluation reviews, just as the captain of a ship keeps constant watch on the compass. Growth check-up is good at any time and should be done regularly by anyone who is working to acquire Christ consciousness, or merely to be happier than he presently is.

So, where were *you*, dear reader, twenty years ago? Were you young and happy, with plans for a good and important future? If so, what became of your plans? Do you today enjoy radiant good health, prosperity that enables you to give greatly? Are you surrounded by people whom you love dearly and who love you? Do you have fewer fears, greater faith, more happiness in living today than you had ten years ago? One year ago?

If you feel that you are actively unhappy for your own soul's sake, you should ask yourself, "Well, what am I going to do about my life from here on?" Make your own self-examination and ask where you really stand in life today. In which way are you headed? Where do you really want to go? What would it take to make you happier than you ever have been? What do you want changed? If you were to come to me with your problems, what would you want me to pray for?

Whatever your self-examination reveals, there is no cause for despair but rather a need for understanding what is wrong, and learning a method of getting yourself headed toward a desired goal. For those who have no real goal but just "want to be happier," I suggest that they set a goal for soul growth. This goal includes many others, and can become a life goal. It leads to becoming a whole, well, and integrated person. Jesus preached a gospel of the whole man.

Our free will can be our own best friend or our worst enemy, according to the way in which we use it. Jesus said a man's enemies were those of his own household, meaning that his emotions, thoughts, words, desires for those often lead to acts against his own best interest. So we need to keep our "household" in line with our goal, accomplish our daily tasks, and achieve happiness. To do this is to grow steadily toward becoming a whole person.

We can profit by a further look at what happiness is and is not. Unhappiness is nature's way of warning us that all is not well with us; if carried to the extreme, it can cause illness and death. Happiness is a basic and good need, and it is more than mere entertainment, fun, or passing the time. Happiness is necessary for soul growth, and soul growth is our purpose for being here on earth, which is a school for man.

For years I have kept track of what makes life worthwhile for different people. What does it take to keep them happy? For scholars and teachers, it nearly always seems to be finding more truth and discovering how to use it for good for themselves and others. Truth (as here used) covers a very wide field of knowledge and works, including history, science, etc. But whether for scholars with degrees, or ordinary people like myself, psychology, history, religion, and many fields of modern science are agreed that happiness is the result of honest accomplishment.

We must note that no amount of pretense of doing and being can bring happiness. It has to be real. People can and do fool others about what they have done, but never can they fool themselves. Again, happiness is the resulting feeling of success—"something attempted, something done." Watch the baby taking his first steps: his success gives him wild joy, happiness. An accomplishment can be as small as learning how to bake a perfect lemon pie, drive a car, do a dance step, grow a garden, or it can be as great as founding a school, a church, a business that will benefit millions and generations. It can be bringing up a child in the way he ought to go, and seeing him become a good, useful and happy person.

My years of working with people with problems, and problem people (there is a great deal of difference between them), have convinced me that there can be little lasting safety or satisfaction for the individual who cannot support himself, make his own way, as we say. Unless he can do things for himself, he feels at the mercy of others and of circumstances beyond his control. Some of the very wealthy people I have worked with, who had never earned a dime, were among the most bitterly and tragically unhappy. They never felt quite safe, always feared that "something might happen" to their money, and often worried lest no one really loved them ("They just cater to me because of my money"). This was especially true of very wealthy women who had married poor men. Many of these non-working wealthy persons had psychosomatic illnesses.

Now, if unearned, piled up money cannot buy good health, love, happiness, or a sense of joy in living, what is the one ingredient that *can* insure happiness in life, by helping us to get things done and so earn happiness? It is the same thing that Jesus had, that which enabled Him to do His works—a sense and absolute knowledge of the fact that He had the power within Himself to do whatever He wanted to do. This knowledge is what gave Jesus His great joy—the joy He wanted to share by

169

teaching others that they had the same power. This kind of joy is properly called the joy of Christ—the Christ consciousness that knows itself, knows its power, knows that it need not depend upon other powers, places, things, or circumstances in order to achieve goals and therefore be safe and happy. Emerson gives us a phrase worthy of remembering, to the effect that "people want power, not candy."

Yes, people do want power. This is why many mistakenly pile up money, thinking it will make them safe, give them power over circumstances and others. This is also why people will eventually want to learn how—I am going to make it stronger, for that is the way I see it—*have to learn how* to use the power of their Word directly, as Jesus did.

Henry David Thoreau wrote that "The mass of men lead lives of quiet desperation." Yes, that is true of the mass of men. But *you* are not a mass of men. You are an individual. Nothing can hold you back but yourself. You can set a very modest goal for yourself—say, to increase your income, or to take a trip around the world, or to get well and stay well. You can then learn how to work with the twelve parts of creative prayer and achieve your goal. Or you can set a goal of becoming a whole person, as we have already discussed. But the highest goal of all, I feel, is that of developing Christ consciousness—the kind of consciousness that uses the power of the Word, under love, directly, as Jesus did.

To the serious student who wants much more information and guidance than this book contains on how to use the power of his Word and work toward a Christ consciousness, I respectfully suggest that he obtain my book *Make Your Dreams Come True.* That book contains all twelve parts of the creative power of prayer. It is the key to my teachings, the method I long have used for myself and taught to my students. (I no longer accept private students, but the earnest searcher will find his way in my books without a teacher.)

"How to Live in the Circle of Prayer and Make Your Dreams Come True," fifth in the order of publication of my books, was first published by Dodd, Mead & Co. in 1959. Unity published it as a serial in one of its magazines, and later brought it out in book form under the title *Make Your Dreams Come True* (which is the title I generally use when lecturing for industry, business, and professional groups). It is the same book, word for word, as originally published and contains the Circle of Prayer chart I created and used with my students for years. It contains case histories from my files, with fourteen chapters of instruction on how to use the Circle of Prayer chart in one's daily life and affairs.

Today science is researching the power of prayer as never before. We know that Jesus lived by prayer and often went alone to pray in the desert or mountains. Dr. Alexis Carrel said of prayer, "It is the only power in the world that seems to overcome the so-called laws of nature." Anyone who has had an instant healing through prayer knows that this is true.

Prayer is a power. All power is locked in law. Prayer power, like that of electricity, travels in a circle. That is why it is "done unto you as you believe," because prayer depends upon faith. Prayer produces after the pattern set, provided we do not break up our prayer pattern with opposite thoughts, words, acts, and so on. The power must work as a whole in all twelve parts. Breaking one part is like pulling out the electric cord that allows the electricity to flow through the clock and move the hands. Disconnecting the power causes all the hours to stop, not just the current one.

My students are asked to keep a record of their individual answered prayers, as a means of building their faith. They are told that praying for others helps create the faith of the world. We, the people of the world, are more closely connected and related than some might imagine. It is true that when we bless others we bless ourselves.

The student who aspires to develop Christ consciousness needs to learn those twelve points of creative prayer, and to know how the twelve work together as a whole. The Circle of Prayer chart is presented in this book on page 8 for your further help.

To those who feel, "There is nothing wrong in my life, it is just the threats of the world of today around me," I want to say:

I believe that by the year 2000 science will have proved so much about the creative power of prayer and the Spiritual laws under which this power operates that millions will be inspired to learn to use the power of the Word. I believe that modern science will announce great truths that will usher in a religious renaissance that will sweep over the world and uplift the spirit of man to heights never before attained.

I am counting on the Truth and New Thought people to keep a record of their answered prayers, and the successful use of the power of their Word. If they will review these records often, they could help to change the spiritual atmosphere of the world for the better. For we know that every thought, feeling, desire, intention of fear, faith, love, hate, anger, or joy goes out from the individual and creates an atmosphere "after its kind." It is a law of nature that one can depend upon and we should use it with a purpose.

Being a life long Methodist and knowing their good works for generations, I cannot praise them too highly. Many of them today study Truth and New Thought literature, as do many from other denominations. All these people together are a powerful force which I think of as *the interim people.* They work ahead of the great average. They hold a certain ground of knowledge, or belief, until others can catch up. No new age could come in without them.

There is another great group of people whom I think of as *the remnant.* They are always present in the world. The Bible speaks of them; they were there, the ones who knew, believed in a better world, a better plan, better people. When the destroyers had done their worst, the remnant moved in to help to start a better world on a higher level. And so today, if worse comes to impossible, if some of the dire predictions of the so-called experts do come true (I feel that they will not), then we will find that help is at hand and has been, from the first.

Then what?

Whether we hold the good we have gained, or take a down dip, progress itself will continue. The human race is always working for that "endless horizon," as Emerson calls it. The soul moves forever outward, upward, onward, for nothing can hold back the evolving soul of man.

So what's to cry? Nothing! If we will learn how correctly and fearlessly to use the power God has given us, we cannot hope too much nor dare too much in this world, or in any world to come.

Oh my brothers, my sisters, let us not stop for one moment but be constant in our belief that a better world, through better people, is at hand. Let us be faithful in our prayers, love, faith, work, and our daily spoken word, so that the new heaven in our hearts will grow and expand and help to build the new world.